CW00595121

£1.50

14/11

ARTHURIANA:

OR,

ESSAYS ON THE ARTHURIAN ROMANCE-CYCLE
AS THE FORMAL MATERIAL OF
THE NEW POESY.

ARTHURIAN LOCALITIES.

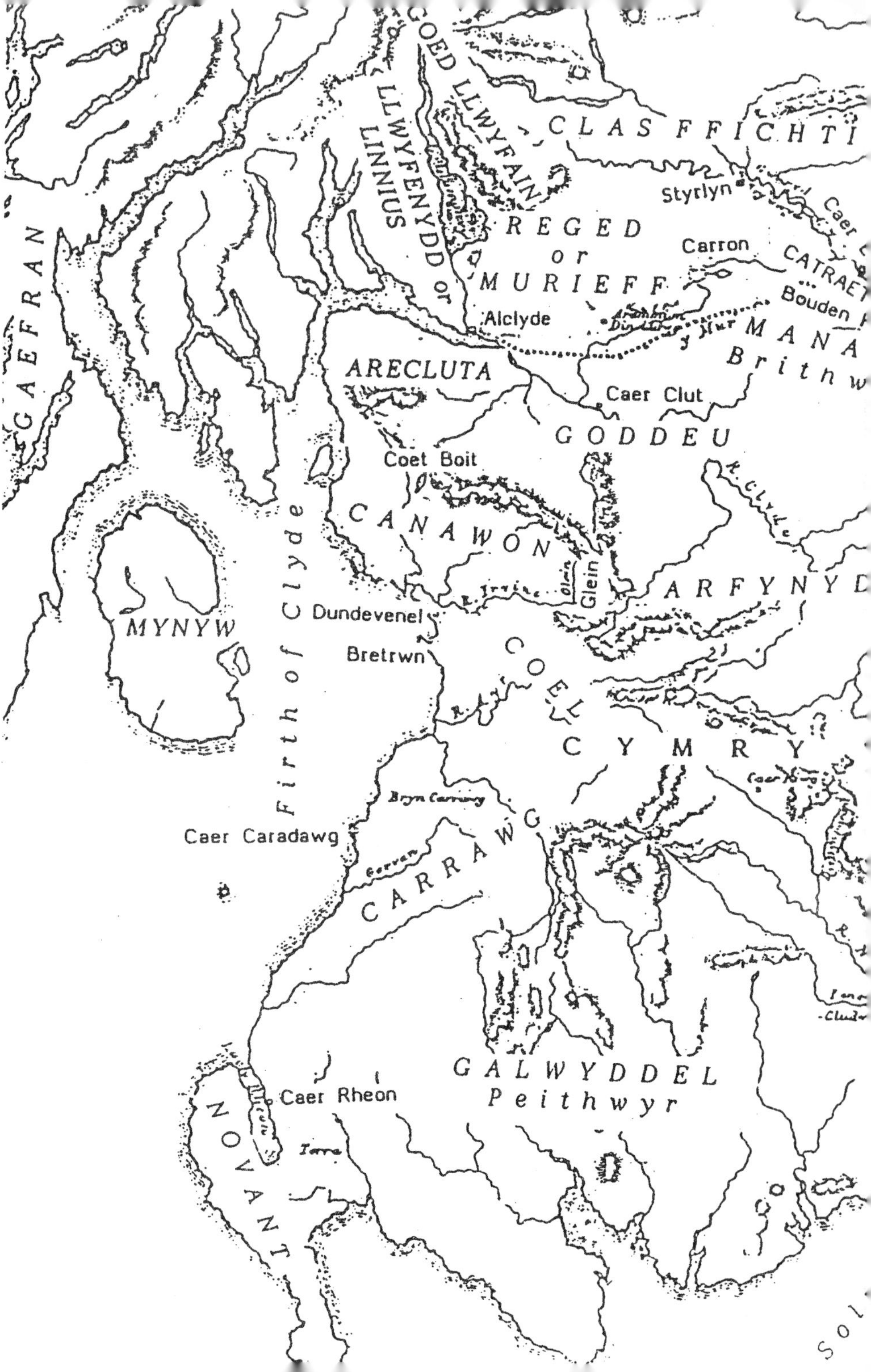
GOED LLWYFAIN
LLWYFENYDD or LINNIUS
CLAS FFICHTI
Styrlyn
REGED or MURIEFF
Carron
CATRAET
Bouden
GAEFRAN
Alclyde
MANA
Brithw
ARECLUTA
Caer Clut
GODDEU
Coet Boit
CANAWON
R. Clyde
Glein
ARFYNYD
MYNYW
Firth of Clyde
Dundevenel
Bretrwn
COEL
CYMRY
Bryn Carrawg
Caer Caradawg
CARRAWG
GALWYDDEL
Peithwyr
Caer Rheon
NOVANT
Sol

Map of PRYDYN
or Y GOGLEDD

Map based on Skene, with minor
modifications.

Firth of Forth

Aberlefdi
.Kepduff
. Dunpender

Mynyd Agned G O D O D I N

D Ó D I N   A n g l e s

Berthmaw

C. Guinion   Wedale

Calchwynyd   Medgaud

COED CELYDDON

— Dinguarey

C Y M R Y   B R Y N E I C H

A n g l e s

B O N

.Erydon

.Ardderyd

Southern Wall

R. Tyne

.char

.h

Caer Lludydd

Publisher's note.

(1) The map of Mr. Stuart Glennie's journeyings is reproduced at the back of this book; the publishers apologize for the reproduction quality. At the front of the book there is a map, based on the one in Skene's *Four Ancient Books*, which was the main source of Mr. Stuart Glennie's information, and which is clearer on some locations.

(2) The views of the author are not necessarily those of the publisher. This book has been reproduced in facsimile because the publishers believe that there is a case for placing at least some of the Arthurian sites in the north of Britain, but it is unlikely that the author is right about all of the sites he gives; in particular, the sitings of Rheged and Catraeth are questionable.

ARTHURIAN LOCALITIES;

THEIR

HISTORICAL ORIGIN, CHIEF COUNTRY, AND FINGALIAN RELATIONS;

WITH A MAP OF

ARTHURIAN SCOTLAND,

BY

JOHN S. STUART GLENNIE, M.A.,
FELLOW OF THE SOCIETY OF ANTIQUARIES;
OF THE ROYAL ASTRONOMICAL SOCIETY, ETC.;
BARRISTER-AT-LAW.

"Sopra la Scozia ultimamente sorse,
Dove la Selva Calidonia appare,
. . . . . .
Gran cose in essa giù fece Tristano,
Lancilotto, Galasso, Artù, e Galvano;
. . . . . .
Restano ancor di più d'una lor pruova
Li monumenti e li trofei pomposi."

ARIOSTO, *Orlando Furioso*, c. IV. ss. 51-2-3

Facsimile reprint by Llanerch Publishers,
Felinfach, 1994. ISBN 1 897853 47 5

1869.

[*All Rights Reserved.*]

PREFACE.

THE germ of the Essay now contributed to the Early English Text Society's Edition of the *Romance of Merlin*, was a paper written in the autumn of 1866, and published under the title of *A Journey through Arthurian Scotland*, in *Macmillan's Magazine* for December, 1867. In this article, I was, I believe, the first to show that Southern Scotland and the English Border is the chief country of Arthurian localities, and to point-out the relation of this district to that of the Fingalian topography of Scotland. I refrained, however, from any affirmation as to whether this district was, or not, the original birthland of Arthurian tradition.

But in the summer of last year, 1868, Mr. Skene published his edition of *The Four Ancient Books of Wales*, in the introduction and notes to which he showed that a large proportion of these poems belonged to the North, and that the historical Arthur was a leader of the Northern Cymry, or the tribes of Southern Scotland and the English Border. Combining, therefore, Mr. Skene's critical results with my own humbler topographical researches, I now for the first time endeavour to prove, after a regularly conducted scientific method, that the district thus indicated is not only the chief country of Arthurian localities, and in interesting relation with that of Fingalian topographical tradition, but also that this district was the original scene of the events of which these localities preserve the mythical traditions. The main Arthurian tradition, therefore,—if the theory of this Essay should be found justified by the evidence brought forward in support of it,—is, in the other districts, where Arthurian localities are to be found, not original, but derived from its birthland in the North.

I have to thank Mr. Pearson, the author of the *History of England in the Early and Middle Ages,* for the very learned note which has enabled me, while combating, to present to my readers, in the fairest possible form, the argument for Arthur as a West-of-England king. To Mr. Pearson, also, my thanks are due for the sight of proofs of his *Historical Maps,* now going through the press. I have likewise to acknowledge the kindness of Mr. Skene, and the courtesy of his publishers, in permitting me to make use of his map of *Prydyn or Y Gogledd* as the basis of mine of *Arthurian Scotland.*

J. S. S-G.

6, Stone Buildings, Lincoln's Inn,
Easter, 1869.

TABLE OF CONTENTS.

ERRATUM.

Two places have, by the engraver's mistake, been named on the Map "Ossian's *Grave*." The place so named in Glencoe should be "Ossian's *Cave*."

ARTHURIAN LOCALITIES;

THEIR HISTORICAL ORIGIN, CHIEF COUNTRY, AND FINGALIAN RELATIONS.

CHAPTER I.

INTRODUCTION---THE OLD ARTHUR-LAND.

ONE of the many indications of that synthetic, and reconstructive, rather than analytic, and destructive, tendency which marks this second half of the nineteenth century is the fact that historical scholars are beginning to look on popular legends and romances, not certainly with the uncritical credulity of the days before Niebuhr, but with the belief of finding in them such records of historical events as will well repay the trouble of investigating them.[1] It seems desirable, therefore, in this introductory chapter, in order at once to indicate the point of view of this Essay, to set-forth, in the first place, the general relation which it seeks to establish between Mediæval Romance and Pre-mediæval History. I shall, then, in the second section, bring before the reader the chief traditional Arthurian Localities of Southern Scotland, Western England, and

[1] See, for instance, DYER, *History of the City of Rome. Introduction.*

North-Western France. After such a survey of the Old Arthur-
land, I shall, in the third section, state the question which I propose
in this Essay more particularly to consider, point-out its interest,
and explain the method by which I hope to attain a definitive
answer. And, in conclusion, I shall state the general subjects of
the succeeding chapters.

SECTION (I).

The Relation of Mediæval Romance to Pre-mediæval History.

The age of the Arthurian, and other great Cycles of Romance, is
that which, in the opinion of both the great thinkers who have
chiefly influenced the intellectual development of Modern Europe,—
in the opinion both of Hegel and of Comte,[2]—began in the eleventh,
and culminated in the thirteenth century. For, about that century,
it is,—as has been conclusively shown by the researches of later
scholars verifying and confirming philosophical speculation,[3]—that
the distinctively Christian, or Catholico-Feudal organization of society attains its highest perfection ; that the Crusades afford their
brightest examples of heroism, and chivalric magnanimity ; that Art
achieves its most original, most variedly beautiful, and majestic
triumphs; and that Literature presents, in the Romances, at once
the highest, and most popular Ideals of the Age. And thus culmi-
nating in the thirteenth century, the Mediæval Age may, as a great
historic period, be defined as the five centuries from the eleventh to
the fifteenth, inclusive. With the sixteenth century begins our

---

[2] " J'aime surtout qu'il (Hegel) ait vu que le monde n'a été vraiment chrétien
qu'au onzième siècle." *Lettre d'A. Comte à M. d'Eichthal* in LITTRÉ, *Auguste
Comte et la Philosophie Positive*, p. 157.

[3] See, for instance, LE CLERC et RENAN, *Histoire Littéraire de la France*, t.
XXIV. *Quatorzième Siècle* (1862)—" Le XIe siècle avait été témoin, en philosophie,
en poésie, en architecture, d'une renaissance comme l'humanité en compte peu dans
ses longs souvenirs. Le XIIe et le XIIIe siècle avaient développé ce germe fécond,
le XIVe et le XVe siècle en avaient vu la décadence." RENAN, *L'Art du Moyen
Age et les Causes de sa Decadence*, in *Revue des Deux Mondes*, t. XL. p. 203 (1862).

present Modern or Transition Age; a period marked, not as was the Mediæval Age, by the general acceptance of an established system of thought, and of government; but a period distinguished by the manifestly progressing destruction of all the political forms, and intellectual foundations of the social system of the Age preceding it, and a no less certain, though perhaps less manifest preparation of a new and higher system of social organization.

But for a thousand years before the opening of the Mediæval Age, Christianity had been working in the European world, completing the destruction of the antique system of thought and of society, and laying the foundations of a new world-system. The first half of this millenium I would distinguish as the Imperial Age. For it is the age of the Roman Empire of the East and West. It is the age also of the Apostles, the Fathers, and the Martyrs of Christianity. And the latter five hundred years of this first millenium of the Christian era I would distinguish as the Barbarian, or Pre-mediæval Age. The Roman Empire no longer extends its sway over Northern and Western Europe; and the various tribes of barbarians,— Celtic and Teutonic,—are engaged in perpetual conflicts,—miserable and disheartening when looked at in their details, but, regarded as a whole, found to be in their great issues conflicts that laid the foundations of the nationalities of a New Europe.[4] For, by the end of this age, there has been constituted in France the first of the Romanic or Neo-Latin nationalities; in England, a preponderatingly Teutonic; and, in Scotland, a predominantly Celtic nationality.[5] And

---

[4] Compare OZANAM, *Civilization au Cinquième Siècle* t. II. p. 315 et seq.

[5] As a writer of such authority as Mommsen has said " Solche Eigenschaften guter Soldaten und schlechter Bürger erklären die geschichtliche Thatsache, dass *die Kelten alle Staaten erschüttert und keinen gegründet haben,*" *(Römische Geschichte* B. IJ., K. IV., b. I., s. 329, *English Translation,* v. I., p. 359), one would not be justified in thus speaking of the consolidation of the tribes of North Britain into a predominantly Celtic nationality without, at least, briefly referring to one's proofs. These are to be found in the unquestionable facts, firstly, that, both in number, and in extent of territory occupied, Celts,—Cymry, Picts and Scots, or Gael,—were the chief basis of the Scotish nationality; secondly, that it was by one of the

·as this Pre-mediæval Age was occupied by the elemental wars of
the tribes ultimately consolidated in these three national unities; so,
the Mediæval Age was filled with the contests of these nations with
each other, and with the rising nationalities around them. But, on
taking a wide view of European history, we shall see these Mediæval
wars preparing, as all conflict does, in fact, prepare, a higher unity.
And, as the name of Scotland is first heard towards the close of the
Pre-mediæval wars of the tribes of North Britain; so, the idea of
Europe emerges from the Mediæval conflict of the races of this
Asiatic promontory.

Now that which, I trust, will be found the most clearly established, as it is the most general view in this Essay maintained, is

Celtic tribes, the Scots, namely, or Gael, that, not only all the other Celtic
elements of the population, but the Saxon element also, was, towards the end of
the Pre-mediæval age, united under one monarch, whose dynasty, or the heirs
of whose dynasty, lost their sovereignty only with the fall of the Stuarts, and
the substitution of the present German Family; and, thirdly, that, in the opinion
of the most competent authorities, not only were the tribes of North Britain thus
united into the Scotish nationality by a Celtic race; not only, that is, have we here,
at least, an exception to what Mommsen declares thus absolutely to be an historical
fact, "that the Celts have shaken all states and have founded none," but the language
of Scotland, both in the Highlands and Lowlands, except a narrow strip of sea-coast,
was, at least till the reign of Malcolm Caenmore (1058-1093), and the opening of the
Mediæval Age, Gaelic. See INNES, *Sketches of Early Scotish History*, pp. 85-6;
compare also ROBERTSON, *Scotland under Her Early Kings*, vol. I., pp. 125, et seq. and
v. II., pp. 142-3, and p. 374; and TYTLER, *History of Scotland*, v. II., p. 188,
et seq. That, during the Mediæval Age, a Teutonic dialect, allied to the English,
took the place of Norman-French, and of Gaelic, at the Court, and further extended
itself in the Lowlands, was due to many causes. Among these, may, for instance,
be named, the marriage of Malcolm Caenmore with the sister of Edgar Atheling, and
the encouragement thence given to the settlement in Scotland of Saxon refugees
from the Norman conquest; the policy of the Scotish monarchs generally in en-
couraging the settlement both of Saxons and Normans, as allies against their own
turbulent subjects; and the naturally preponderating influence of the inhabitants of
sea-coasts. See note 16 *infrà* p. 27. And yet to this hour one may, in a day's
journey from such a vast centre of an English-speaking population as Glasgow,
find the simplest English question answered with "No English!" Celts *have*,
therefore, once, at least, succeeded in *founding*, though not in long maintaining,
a state with a purely Celtic organization and language. But have Saxons founded
or long maintained a State with a purely Teutonic organization? These current
generalizations about the Celts will seldom bear being strictly examined. See
ROBERTSON, as above, *Appendix B. The Celt and the Teuton*, v. II. p. 197 et seq.

that in the Romances of the Mediæval Age, and more particularly in
those of the Arthurian Cycle, there is not only a mythological
element, as I hope in another Essay fully to show ; but that
there is a very important historical element ; a record, legendary
indeed, and hardly to be deciphered for its extraordinary flourishes,
but still a record of certain real, and not purely fictitious characters, incidents, and conflicts of the Premediæval Age. And
if this should be established, we shall certainly have a result
which will reward the labour of this investigation of Arthurian
localities ; a result not only for the general Mediæval history
of European literature ; but for the Pre-mediæval history of
that particular region in which our researches may localize the
events from which the historic element of the Arthurian Romances
is derived. Of no slight historic interest can it be to show that
Arthur and Merlin are neither purely mythic personages, nor mere
poetic creations ; but that the legends and traditions that the
Mediæval trouveres and troubadours wrought-out into their magnificent romances, were records of actual Pre-mediæval personages, whose characters and histories had forcibly impressed the
popular imagination ; and that the country where the heroic Arthur
fought, and the forests where the wild Merlin wandered, can be
now, on no doubtful evidence, pointed-out. The one, no doubt, was
but a leader of barbarians, and the other but a barbarian compound
of madman and poet, of prophet and bard. But it is these very circumstances that give their characters an historic interest in relation
to their Mediæval idealisation.

　　And not only shall we thus see the Mediæval connected with the
Pre-mediæval Age in the relation between the Romantic Ideals of
the one, and the Traditional Heroes of the other ; but, in showing
that the Mediæval Romances had an historic element, and that the
age and country of those characters who lived-again in the Romantic
Ideals, can be now assigned ; we shall connect also with that Pre-

mediæval, our present Modern Age. For there are many indications, not only in the needs of the time, and in the characteristic advantages of the Arthurian Mythology; but in the actual fact of the use already made of it by so many modern poets; [6] that the Mediæval Romances of King Arthur will be the chief formal material of the New Poesy. To show, therefore, that these Mediæval Romances had in them a definite historical element, is to give that New Poesy also an historic basis; to discover for its characters and incidents " a local habitation ;" and to connect by a new bond the Present, not only with the Mediæval, but with the Pre-mediæval Age.

Another, a still higher, a moral interest this investigation seems also to me to have; and I trust that, before entering upon it, I may be pardoned for alluding for a moment to these higher, these moral aspects of our subject. Let me but desire my readers to reflect how the establishment of such a relation, as will here occupy us, between Mediæval Romance and Pre-mediæval history, brings home the great idea of the continuity of human development; how it shows the traditions of the barbarian conflicts of one age taken up by the next, and used as the formal material of the creations of a magnificent poesy; how it shows the rude lives of an earlier period living again in the ideal heroes of succeeding ages; how it shows that, though the tribes of whom these traditions are the historic memorials, were conquered, absorbed and extinguished as separate political organizations, yet they died not; how it shows that, in the succession of Humanital, as in the sequence of Natural phenomena, there is, in fact, no such thing as Death; that there is but Decease only, and Transformation. And thus it is but a great historic truth mythically expressed, that legend of Merlin's prophecies from his Tomb. "Lady," replied Merlin, "the flesh upon me will be rotten

---

[6] I need here only recall Mr. Tennyson's *Idylls of the King*, Mr. Arnold's *Tristram and Iseult*, Mr. Morris's *Defence of Guenivere*, Edgar Quinet's epic *Merlin*, and Richard Wagner's "Poèmes d'Opera," *Lohengrin*, and *Tristan et Iseult.*

before a month shall have past; but my spirit will not be wanting
to all those who shall come here."[7]

> " Vive la voce; e come chiara emerga,
> Udir potrai da la marmorea tomba;
> Che le passate e le future cose,
> A chi gli domandò sempre rispose." [8]

SECTION (II).

The Arthurian Localities of Southern Scotland, Western England, and
North-Western France.

Let us now proceed to our preliminary survey of the traditional
Arthur-land. Localities with Arthurian names, or Arthurian traditions attached to them, are to be found, in greater or less abundance,
in Scotland, in Wales, Somersetshire, and Cornwall, and in Brittany.
In Scotland, there is still pointed out in the churchyard of Meigle, on
the borders of Perthshire and Forfarshire, an ancient sculptured stone
said to mark "Ganore's Grave," or the tomb of Guenivere. Arthur's
Seat still connects Edinburgh with the mythic hero's fame. And
at Drummelziar on the Tweed is still to be seen the perennial
thorn that has not yet ceased, in an offshoot at least, to bloom over
the grave of Merlin. How many more Arthurian localities are to
be found in Scotland will, in the third chapter of this essay, be
shown in detail. Postponing, then, any further notice of the
Arthurian localities of Southern Scotland, I shall at once proceed
to those of Western England.

In North Wales, between Mold and Ruthin, near Colomendy
Lodge, in Flintshire, is Maen Arthur, a stone which, in popular
fancy, bears an impression of the hoof of the hero's steed.
Between Mold and Denbigh is Moel Arthur, an ancient British
fort, defended by two ditches of great depth. Near Denbigh,
"there is, in the Paroch of *Llansannan* in the Side of a Stony
Hille, a Place wher there be 24 Holes or Places in a Roundel
for Men to sitte in, but sum lesse, and some bigger, cutte oute of

---

[7] *Prophecies de Merlin*, F. 76.   [8] ARIOSTO, *Orlando Furioso*, c. III. s. 11.

the mayne Rok by Mannes Hand; and there Children and Young
Men cumming to seke their Catelle use to sitte & play. Sum caulle
it *the Rounde Table.* Kiddes use ther communely to play & skip
from Sete to Sete."[9] The remains of what would appear to have
been a Roman Camp overlooking Redwharf Bay, or Traeth Coch,
in Anglesea, is locally called Burdd Arthur, or Arthur's Round
Table. Also in Anglesey, in the grounds of Llwydiarth, a seat of
the Lloyd family, is a famous Maen Chwf, or rocking stone, called
Arthur's Quoit. In Caernarvonshire, to the south of Snowdon, "overlooking the lower end of Llyn y Ddinas, is Dinas Emrys, a singular
isolated rock, clothed on all sides with wood, containing on the
summit some faint remains of a building defended by ramparts,"
with which a legend of Merlin and Vortigern is connected :—

> " And from the top of Brith, so high and wondrous steep,
>   Where Dinas Emris stood, shewed where the serpents fought,
>   The White that tore the Red; from whence the prophet wrought
>   The Briton's sad decay then shortly to ensue."[10]

In this same county, at Llyn Geirionydd, as also at Aberystwith,
and other localities on the Cardiganshire coast, Taliessin, another of
the four great bards of the sixth century, is said to have been found
on the shore, like Moses in the bulrushes, by Gwyddno Garanhir.[11]
And, on the south of Caernarvon Bay, is Nant Gwrtheyrn, the
Hollow of Vortigern, a precipitous ravine by the sea, said to have
been the last resting place of the usurper,—so, at least, he is represented in the *Romance of Merlin*,[12]—when he fled to escape the rage
of his subjects on finding themselves betrayed to the Saxons. In
Merionethshire, there is a river with the Arthurian name of Camlan
flowing into the Eden. And the Church of Llanover, near the
Bala Lake in this county, is said to have been the burial place of

---

[9] LELAND, *Itinerary*, v. V. pp. 62, 63.
[10] DRAYTON, *Poly-Olbion, Song the Tenth. Works*, v. III. p. 843.
[11] GUEST (Lady Charlotte), *The Mabinogion*, v. III. p. 360.
[12] Chapters II. and III. (Early English Text Society).

one of the four most famous bards of the Arthurian Age, Llywarch Hen, or Llywarch, the Aged. To the address of this bard to his Crutch Mr. Arnold refers in illustration of "the Titanism of the Celt, his passionate, turbulent, indomitable reaction against the despotism of fact." [13]

"O my Crutch! is it not the first day of May? The furrows, are they not shining? The young corn, is it not springing? Ah! the sight of thy handle makes me wroth."

In South Wales, near the turnpike road from Reynoldstone to Swansea, on the north slope of Cefn Bryn, there is the famous cromlech called Arthur's Stone. About five miles to the south of Brecon on the Usk, rise the twin peaks of the Beacons called Arthur's Chair. On an eminence adjoining the park of Mocras Court, in Brecknockshire, is a large and peculiar kind of British cromlech, called Arthur's Table. And at the once famous city, now the decayed village, of Caerleon upon Usk,—the *Isca Silurum* of Antoninus, where the second Augustan Legion was, during a long period, in garrison,—are the remains of a Roman Amphitheatre, in a bank of earth heaped up in an oval form sixteen feet high, and now also called Arthur's Round Table. Some four miles from Caermarthen, itself said to be derived, but quite erroneously,[14] from Caer Merddin, the city of Merlin, is Merlin's Grove, and Hill. And on the bank of the Towy, within the domain of Dynevor Park, Spenser has placed the cave of Merlin :—

> "There the wise Merlin, whilom wont, they say,
>   To make his wonne low underneath the ground,
> In a deep delve far from the view of day,
>   That of no living wight he might be found,
>   When so he counselled with his sprights around.
>   . . . .

---

[13] *On the Study of Celtic Literature*, p 155. See also *Four Ancient Books*, v. I. p. 326.

[14] NASH, *Merlin the Enchanter and Merlin the Bard*, p. x. Caer Myrdin, or Merddin is a Welsh corruption of the Roman *Mari-dunum*, "Sea-town." Compare SELDEN's Note on the Fourth Song of Drayton's *Poly-Olbion*, Works, v. II. p. 746, and v. III. p. 852.

> It is a hideous, hollow, cave-like bay,
> Under a rock that has a little space
> From the swift Tyvi, tumbling down apace
> Amongst the woody hills of Dynevowr." [15]

In Somersetshire, may first be mentioned Bath, the *Aquæ Solis* or *Sulis* of the Romans. But the reasons against here localizing the Arthurian Battle of Badon Hill mentioned by Nennius are well stated by Dr. Guest,[16] though, as will be seen hereafter, I cannot agree with his suggestion, " Why may not the Mons Badonicus be the Badbury of Dorsetshire?"[17] Between Castle Cary and Yeovil, on the escarpment of the oolite, abutting on the plain which extends to Ilchester, is Cadbury, " a hill of a mile compass at the top, four trenches encircling it, and twixt every of them an earthen wall; the content of it, within about twenty acres full of ruins and reliques of old buildings. . . . . 'Dii boni (saith Leland) quot hîc profundissimarum fossarum? quot hîc egestæ terræ valla? quæ demum præcipitia? atque ut paucis finiam, videtur mihi quidem esse et Artis et Naturæ miraculum.' Antique report makes this one of Arthur's places of his Round Table."[18] Cadbury is mentioned in old records under the name of Camelot, a name still perpetuated in the adjoining villages of Queen's Camel and West Camel. In the fourth ditch is a spring called King Arthur's Well. And the relics found in the fortress prove it to have been occupied by the Romans, though, as we have seen, tradition assigns its origin to King Arthur, who, in the opinion of Camden, probably fought a battle with the Saxons in this neighbourhood. The other famous Arthurian locality of Somersetshire is Glastonbury, which, once encircled by the arms of the Brue, or Brent, formed the Roman Insula Avalonia, or Isle of Avalon.

---

[15] " *Faerie Queene*," iii. 3. Compare also DRAYTON, *Poly-Olbion, Song the Fifth* Works, v. II. pp. 756-7.

[16] *Early English Settlements in South Britain*, p. 35.

[17] Ibid. p. 36.

[18] SELDEN, Note on Drayton's *Poly-Olbion, Works*, v. II. p. 724.

"O three times famous Isle, where is that place that might
 Be with thyself compared for glory and delight,
 Whilst Glastenbury stood ? exalted to that pride,
 Whose monastery seemed all other to deride.

. . . .

To whom didst thou commit that monument to keep
 When not Great Arthur's tomb, nor holy Joseph's grave,
 From sacrilege had power their holy bones to save ?"[19]

Selden's annotation on this passage seems worth giving, at least
in part. "Henry the Second in his expedition towards Ireland enter-
tained by the way in Wales with bardish songs, wherein he heard it
affirmed that in Glastonbury (made almost an isle by the river's
embracements) Arthur was buried betwixt two pillars, gave com-
mandment to Henry of Blois, then abbot, to make search for the
corps, which was found in a wooden coffin (Girald saith oaken,
Leland thinks alder), some sixteen foot deep ; but after they had
digged nine foot, they found a stone on whose lower side was fixt
a leaden cross (crosses fixt upon the tombs of old Christians were
in all places ordinary) with his name inscribed, and the letter side
of it turned to the stone. He was then honoured with a sumptuous
monument, and afterwards the sculls of him and his wife Guinever
were taken out (to remain as separate relics and spectacles) by
Edward Longshanks and Eleanor . . . . Worthily famous was the
Abbey also from Joseph of Arimathea (that Εὐσχήμων βουλητὴς,
as S. Mark calls him) here buried, etc."[20] But, notwithstanding
the inscription on the leaden cross, "Hic jacet sepultus inclytus rex
Arthurus in insula Avalonia ; " or as it is otherwise more epigram-
matically given, "Hic jacet Arthurus, Rex quondam, Rexque fu-
turus ; "—

"His Epitaph recordeth so certaine
 Here lieth K. Arthur that shall raigne againe ;—"[21]

it is hardly necessary to add that there is almost every reason to

[19] Drayton, Poly-Olbion, Song the Third, Works, v. II. p. 712.
[20] Ibid. v. II. p. 722.
[21] Lidgate, Boccace Lib. VIII. Cap. 24.

believe that this extraordinary " find" could have been nothing but a pious fraud, *in majorem monasterii gloriam.*[22]

In Cornwall (*Cornu Galliæ*), Camelford and Tintagel have a pre-eminence in Arthurian tradition similar to that maintained by Cadbury and Glastonbury in Somersetshire. Not far from Camelford is a little entrenchment, known as Arthur's Hall. On the Camel or Alan (*Crum hayle*, crooked river) the final battle is said to have been fought between Arthur and his rebellious nephew, or rather, bastard son, Mordred.

> " Let Camel of her course & curious windings boast,
> . . . .
> . . . . her proper course that loosly doth neglect,
> As frantic, ever since her British Arthur's blood,
> By Mordred's murtherous hand was mingled with her flood."[23]

Between Camelford and Launceston, on Wilsey Downs, is Warbelow Barrow, an ancient fortification of considerable size, in the centre of which is a large mound, popularly called King Arthur's Grave. At Slaughter Bridge, between Camelford and Tintagel, on the Bristol Channel, a stone, with the hero's name on it, is pointed out. Tintagel, though in the romances of Sir Tristrem it is made the Castle of King Mark, is the reputed birthplace and residence of Arthur.[24] Some of the rock basins in the slate of the promontory are fantastically called King Arthur's Cups and Saucers; and south of Tintagel, near St. Colomb, is the eminence of Castle an Dinas, or the earth-fort, crowned with an elliptical doubly entrenched camp of six acres, which tradition affirms to have been the hunting-seat of King Arthur, who, according to the legends, chased the wild deer on the Tregon Moors. Some miles north of Liskeard are several rocky tors, one group of which is called King Arthur's Bed (*Beth*, *i.e.*, Grave ?). Lyonnesse, the possession of Sir Tristrem, is said

---

[22] See, however, Mr. Pearson's note, *infrà*, p. 136.

[23] DRAYTON, *Poly-Olbion, Song the First, Works,* v. II. p. 660.

[24] An account of a recent visit to it is given by the author of *John Halifax* in *Good Words* for January, 1867; *In King Arthur's Land; a Week's Study of Cornish Life.* Jennifer (Guenivere ?) is mentioned as a common name.

to have been that submerged tract of slate by which the Scilly Isles, the outlying members of that series of granitic highlands which extends through Cornwall to Dartmoor, were traditionally united to the mainland; and two of the most eastern isles of this little archipelago are distinguished by the names of Great, and Little Arthur.

Crossing the Channel, we find in Little Britain, or Brittany, another district boasting itself to be the cradle of romance. In the Cornuailles and Leonais, two of its ancient divisions, we have another Cornwall and Lyonnesse. In the latter, is situated Kerduel, where Arthur is said to have held his Court. A short distance off the coast is the island of Aiguilon or Avalon, where, as in the Insula Avalonia of Glastonbury, he is said to have been buried. And near this also is Mount St. Michael, with its legend of the hero's rescue of the fair Helena, the niece of Hoel, from the hateful embraces of the giant.

> " . . . . great Rython's self he slew in his repair
> Who ravish'd Howell's niece, young Heliena the fair;
> And for a trophy brought the giant's coat away,
> Made of the beards of kings." [25]

"On the banks of the Elorn are still pointed out the sites of the castles and forts of Launcelot du Lac, and of La Blonde Yseult. In the Morbihan, the next Celtic division to that of Cornuailles, is shown the Forest of Broceliande, where Merlin ' drees his weird ;' and there also is the consecrated fountain of Balanton, which is still believed to possess miraculous properties. There also may be found Caradoc and Madoc, and other names peculiar to the ancient legends of British History." [26]

SECTION (III).

The Question proposed, its Interest, and the Method of its Solution.

Thus we find Arthurian localities in all the five districts, in modern times known as Southern Scotland, Wales, Somersetshire,

[25] DRAYTON, *Poly-Olbion, Song the Fourth, Works,* v. II. p. 735.
[26] FORBES-LESLIE, *The Early Races of Scotland and their Monuments,* v. I. p. 12.

Cornwall, and Brittany. And hence the first result of a general inquiry into Arthurian topography is the outlining of a continuous region from the Grampians, in Scotland, to the Loire, in France, distinguished by localities with Arthurian names, or Arthurian traditions attached to them. This region may be briefly described as including what is now the south of Scotland, the west of England, and the northwest of France.[27] And the question which I propose in this Essay mainly to consider, and, if possible, definitively to answer, is :—Which of these three divisions of the old Arthur-land, that of Scotland, of England, or of France, was the original birthland of Arthurian tradition ?

To show the importance of this question, and to excite an interest in its solution, I trust that the following brief remarks will be sufficient. In the first place, then, it opens up to the philosophic historian the general question of the origin of traditional topographies ; a question which has not only not been, as yet, so far as I am aware, treated scientifically, except with respect to some of the Syrian localities of Christian tradition; but which is connected in its general bearings with all those other questions of origin which so directly affect the validity of popular religious beliefs. But, farther, it is an inquiry, the result of which will be to draw back the veil from ancient centuries of the history of mankind, and to connect, with still existing monuments, long past events of that struggle for existence, which, of all others, must chiefly interest us of the human race.

But, besides these general results, the inquiry on which we would now enter, ought, at length, to present us with the local historical

---

[27] Arthurian traditions, it must, however, be noted, attach also to some places beyond the limits of the region thus described, and rather in the south, than the west of England. For instance,

" And for great Arthur's seat, her Winchester prefers,
  Whose old Round Table yet she vaunteth to be hers;"

sings Drayton in the Second Song of the *Poly-Olbion*, so often above quoted (*Works*, v. II. p. 691).

basis of that vast cycle of Romance the large place of which in the
history of European literature, and the great influence of which on
the development of modern civilization, is now more or less fully
acknowledged. Yet, further, if I am right in the conclusion that
the two chief elements determining the form of the Mediæval
Arthurian Romances are to be found in historical events of the
Premediæval Age, and in Celtic myths, which may be traced back
to the earliest forms of speech distinctive of the Indo-European
Races,[28] this inquiry will appear as the necessary preliminary to the
investigation of the Arthurian branch of a mythology which is
second in interest only to that which has gathered round the historical facts of Christian tradition. And yet, further, if, as seems
probable, not only from their special characteristics, but from the
use increasingly made of them, the Arthurian Romances are destined to become the chief formal material of European poesy ;
such an inquiry as the following should, in determining the original locality of Arthurian tradition, fix also the site of a new
classic land, in which, as of old, in Greece, the creations of poesy
in all its different forms, may have a common "local habitation,"
and gain all the advantages, thus only given, of vivid realization in
the popular fancy.

   For those to whom the force of these considerations in illustration of the importance of the question above proposed, and the
interest of its solution, may not be at once apparent, let me add,
what may to some antiquarians be the most stimulating circumstances of all, the facts, simply, that this question has been
eagerly discussed ; that the answer here given, though it has been
suggested, cannot be held to have been hitherto proved ;[29] and that

----

[28] In the same way as the linguistic origin of the Classic myths has been explained
by modern philology. See MAX MÜLLER, *Lectures on the Science of Language,* and
Chips from a German Workshop.

[29] Chalmers remarks that "the valourous Arthur of History and the redoubtable
Arthur of Romance has supplied the topography of North Britain with such signi-

the method of proof which has been followed is new, inasmuch

ficant names, as seem to imply, either that the influence of the real Arthur was felt, or the remembrance of the fictitious Arthur was preserved, for many ages after the Pendragon had fallen by the insidious stroke of treachery from the kindred hand of Mordred." *Caledonia*, v. I. p. 244. Sir Walter Scott, in a note on his *Vision of Don Roderick, Introduction*, s. iv., observes that "much of the ancient poetry preserved in Wales refers less to the history of the Principality to which that name is now limited, than to events which happened in the north-west of England, and south-west of Scotland, where the Britons for a long time made a stand against the Saxons." And he further refers to the connection of Aneurin, Llywarch Hen, and Merlin with Scotland rather than with Wales. Compare also his introduction to *Sir Tristrem*, pp. xxxiv-viii. ; and to *Thomas the Rhymer*, Part II. in *Minstrelsy of the Scotish Border*. A writer in the *Gentleman's Magazine* of 1842 was, however, the first, I believe, distinctly to maintain that "the seat of Arthur's power was . . . . . adjacent to the Saxon settlement of Lothian;" and that "in connection with that settlement his victories are recorded by Nennius." And he adds that the mistake of assigning to Arthur a kingdom in the south-western extremity of the island "was possibly confirmed by the casual similarity of name between Arthur's real subjects in the north, and those assumed for him in the Cornish promontory, the former bearing the designation of Damnii, the latter of Dumnonii" v. XVII. p. 486. But the incompleteness of the evidence advanced in support of this conclusion was probably the reason of its attracting but little attention. Mr. Nash also asserts, but does not even attempt to prove a theory similar to that in this essay maintained. "The original locality," he says, "of the traditions which have furnished the groundwork of these world-renowned romances (of King Arthur) is probably the Cumbrian region taken in its widest extent from the Firths of Forth and Clyde southward and westward along the borders of the Northumbrian kingdom, in which the famous exploits of the British Cymric struggle with the Northumbrian Angles became the theme of a native minstrelsy, transplanted into Brittany by the refugees from the Saxon conquest, and moulded into the romances with which we have been made acquainted by the Norman trouveres." *Merlin the Enchanter and Merlin the Bard*, p. iv. And Mr. Burton at least admits that, "if any reality could be extracted from the Arthurian histories, Scotland would have its full share, since much of the narrative comes northward of the present border." *History of Scotland*, v. I. pp. 174-7. On the other hand, however, Dr. Guest identifies Arthur with Owen Finddu, the son of Aurelius Ambrosius, and places him in the south-west of England ; remarking that his being called the son of Uter arose from Geoffrey of Monmouth's having mistaken the meaning of the term applied to him by Nennius, *map uter*, "the terrible boy, because he was cruel from his childhood." *Welsh and English Rule in Somersetshire after the Capture of Bath*, A.D. 577. *Archæological Journal*, 1859, p. 123 et seq. And Mr. Pearson also makes Arthur sovereign of a territory in the south-west of England of which Camelot, or Cadbury, in Somersetshire, was the capital. *Early and Middle Ages of England*, v. I. p. 56-8. See also *Bishop Percy's Folio Manuscript*, v. I. pp. 401-4 ; and *infrà* p. 133. And Col. Forbes-Leslie, without appearing to have a suspicion that Scotland may be the true birthland of Arthurian tradition, says : " I do not presume to give an opinion on the rival claims of Wales, Cornwall, and Armorica, to the domicile of King Arthur and his Paladins, and Merlin with his magical powers.' *Early Races of Scotland and their Monuments*, v. I. p. 167 (1866).

as it is an adaptation of physical methods to antiquarian researches.

That method has consisted, first, in examining the results of the
modern scientific criticism of Celtic history, political, and literary,
in as far as these results more particularly bear on the definite
localization of events which may have been the origin of those
traditions which, in our investigation of Arthurian topography, we
have found to be so widely diffused. Our deduction from these
critical results has been that it was in Southern Scotland, and
neither in Western England, nor in North-western France that
the Arthurian traditions, still attached to so much of the topography of all these districts, originated. This deduction, however,
standing alone, could hardly in any case, and especially considering
the scantiness of the materials on which it is founded, be received as
satisfactory scientific proof of the historical origin of Arthurian
localities. And hence the necessity of an inductive verification of
our deductive theory. How was such a verification to be gained?

By the second step of the method which has guided these researches. This was founded on the postulate, or assumption, that,
except special reasons could be shown to the contrary, that district
in which the Arthurian traditions had their local historical origin
would be found to be the chief country of Arthurian localities. I
therefore noted, in the course of a great many perambulations of
the region thus critically indicated, all the localities there to be
found with Arthurian names, or Arthurian traditions attached to
them. The general result of these journeys was a determination of
that district of Southern Scotland and the English Border, in which
the Arthurian traditions had, according to our critical theory, had their
local origin, as, to this day, the chief country of Arthurian localities.
This, on the principle above stated, I seemed justified in regarding
as the required inductive verification. And thus it is in the fact
of the accordance of the deduction from the results of literary and

historical criticism, with the induction from the results of topographical investigation, that the main proof of the thesis in this essay maintained, namely, that Scotland is the original seat of Arthurian tradition, consists.

But our conclusions both as to the historical origin and the chief country of the Arthurian localities, having been found to be thus accordant and mutually confirmatory in their indication of Southern Scotland, it did not appear that our investigation would be scientifically complete without an examination of the relations of the Scotish Arthurian topography to that Fingalian topography which has been long known to be possessed by Scotland, as well as Ireland. Nor will, I trust, this third step in our investigation of Arthurian localities be thought other than a necessary part of our discussion of Arthurian localities, if, instructed by the results of that most powerful of modern scientific instruments, the Comparative Method, one has been led to see how necessary is the study of the Fingalian Myths in the scientific investigation of the Arthurian Romances; if one considers the importance of the fact that the local relations, discovered in Scotland, of Arthurian to Fingalian tradition, are nowhere else to be found ; and if, especially, I am successful in showing in these unique relations a confirmation of the theory here maintained as to the original birthland of the traditions of King Arthur.

Having thus, in this first, or introductory chapter, set-forth the general relation which I seek to establish between Mediæval Romance and Pre-mediæval History ; having briefly noted the chief traditional localities of the Old Arthur-land, considered as a continuous European region; and having stated the method by which I propose to determine the special district in which Arthurian traditions originated, the subjects of the succeeding chapters will be as follows. In the next, or second chapter, those results of the criticism of Cymric history will be detailed, from which the deduction, as to the origin of Arthurian localities, is drawn. In the third chapter, a summary account will be given of the very numerous perambulations of the Arthurian district of Scotland, from the result of which arises the verificative induction as to the chief country of Arthurian localities. In the fourth chapter it will be shown how variously suggestive, and confirmatory of the conclusions of the foregoing chapters, are those Fingalian relations of the Arthurian topography of Scotland, presented by the examination of Pictish memorials. And, fifthly, I shall, in conclusion, briefly advert to considerations that should seem to give more than merely antiquarian interest to this discovery of the true, or original country of Arthurian tradition.

Let me now, then, endeavour to show that that part of those far Islands of the West where terminated, until their new exodus in the present age,[30] and where were reunited, at length, the two great northern and southern streams of Celtic migration from the Asian birthland of the Aryan tribes;—that part of the Old Arthur-land in which the Pre-mediæval events which are the chief historical bases of the Arthurian Romances of the Mediæval trouveres and troubadours actually occurred, and where the tradition of these events has to this day the most numerous topographical monuments;—is that district of the largest of the British Isles which, bounded on the north by the chain of the Grampians, and on the south by the Tyne and the Derwent, was formerly known as *Y Gogledd,* or "the North," and which I would distinguish as Arthurian Scotland.[31]

[30] See BURY (Lord), *Exodus of the Western Nations.*

[31] This term is thus used to include part of what is now England. But, I think, justifiably: not only because it is a more convenient, though, perhaps, less exact term than "Southern Scotland and the English Border;" but because the dominion of the early Scotish kings extended, though precariously, beyond the present border; and because Cumberland and Northumberland were not finally annexed to the Crown of England till the third of Henry II. See HINDE, *On the Early History of Cumberland,* in *The Archæological Journal,* 1859, p. 217 et seq.

Let me, now,—but without any assumption, in so obscure a matter, of absolutely proving my case,—bring forward in due order those results of critical and topographical research which appear to me to support each other in the conclusion that Southern Scotland and the English Border is the true historical region of the Old Arthur-land.

CHAPTER II.

THE HISTORICAL ORIGIN OF ARTHURIAN LOCALITIES AS DEDUCED FROM THE CRITICISM OF CYMRIC HISTORY.

IN attempting to answer the question before us as to the birth-land of Arthurian tradition, I shall, in this chapter, briefly state those results of a critical examination of Cymric history, political and literary, from which we seem justified in concluding—first, that the Arthur of the earliest historical sources, and of the earliest bardic poems, was a leader of the northern Cymry, and, hence, that the North was the cradle of Arthurian story; secondly, that, in the history of the northern Cymry, there were conditions inimical to the importation and preservation of Arthurian traditions, supposing they did *not* originate in the North in an historical Arthur; and thirdly, that, on the other hand, in the history of the southern Cymry, there were conditions in the highest degree favourable to the importation of Arthurian traditions, supposing they *had* in the North, their historical origin. It is but just to add that I shall found these conclusions principally on the results of the admirable Celtic researches of Mr. Skene.[1]

SECTION (I).

Direct Indications of the North as the Historical Birthland of Arthurian Tradition.

First, then, let me state those critical results which directly

---

[1] Chiefly as contained in his Introductions, or Prefaces, to *The Four Ancient Books of Wales*, *The Book of the Dean of Lismore*, and *The Chronicles of the Picts and Scots*.

indicate the North as the birthland of Arthurian tradition. This I shall do in the order of the questions that logically arise in an investigation of Cymric history. The first of these is as to the number and character of the earliest authentic sources of such history? Besides the old Roman and Saxon authorities, these sources are but three in number—first, the *Historia* and *Epistola* of Gildas which, from internal evidence, appears to have been composed in the year 560; secondly, the works which go under the name of Nennius, of which the first would appear to have been written in the seventh century, soon after the *Origines* of Isidore of Seville who died in 636, and the others in the succeeding centuries, down to 1072; thirdly, the *Ancient Laws and Institutes of Wales*, of which the oldest, the Laws of Howel dda, are of the tenth century.

We have next to inquire what, so far as we can gather it from these ancient historical sources, was the distribution of the Cymric population in the sixth century, the earliest of which we find native historians? And we thence discover that, instead of the Cymry being, as commonly supposed, confined to Wales and Cornwall, with the Picts and Scots occupying the country to the north of the wall between the Tyne and the Solway; the Cymry possess the whole of the country from the Dee and the Humber to the Firths of Forth and Clyde, except the east coast from the Tyne to the Esk, where the Saxons are gradually encroaching, and the district of Galloway on the north of the Solway, between the Nith and Loch Ryan, where the Picts still maintain themselves. But while we are thus shown the Cymric population extending much further north than we have hitherto generally believed, we find also that, instead of Wales being exclusively occupied by Cymry, its western seaboard is in the possession of the Gwyddyl, or Gael, (Scots from Ireland?) a line drawn from Conway, on the north, to Swansea on the south, separating the two (Celtic) races of the

Gwyddyl and the Cymry, on the west and on the east.[2] Further, as to the distribution of the Cymry in this early period, it seems here necessary only to add that the Bretons of Armorica were of this race;[3] as also should seem to have been the Belgæ of Holland, Belgium, Flanders, Picardy, and Normandy, by this time, however, for the most part absorbed by a Teutonic population.[4] Thus, as the first important result of our historical criticism, we find that the region in which, as has, in the foregoing chapter been shown, Arthurian localities are now to be found, is co-extensive with that occupied in the sixth century by the Cymric race.

On what part of this extensive territory did the events recorded by the earliest historians of the Cymry take place? The answer given by Mr. Skene, as the result of his examination of the above-mentioned sources, and particularly of the *Historia Britonum*, the earliest of the works collected under the name of Nennius, is— that these earliest recorded events occurred in the north of this Cymric territory, in those petty states or kingdoms of Strathclyde and Cumbria, which now form the south of Scotland and the English Border. `And the Arthur of Nennius, the only historic Arthur, thus appears as the *dux bellorum* or *Guledig* of these northern Cymric states in a prolonged, but victorious conflict with the Saxons of the Bernician kingdom of the eastern coast, and the Picts from the other side of the Forth, in the sixth century. For the detailed proof of this very important conclusion, I shall here only refer to Mr. Skene's recent work; to those papers in the *Gentleman's Magazine* of 1842, above referred to (p. xvii[o]. n. 21), which, maintaining a similar theory, first, I believe, suggested to Mr. Skene the course of research, of which we have the ripe fruit in the *Four Ancient Books;* and to the Appendix to this Essay.

[2] *Four Ancient Books* v. I. p. 43. See also Jones (Archdeacon), *Vestiges of the Gael in Gwynedd.*
[3] Souvestre, *Les Derniers Bretons*, v. I. p. 144.
[4] Nichols' *Pedigree of the English*, p. 40.

The early distribution of the Cymric race, and the place of the earliest events recorded by its historians, being thus determined, the way is cleared for an answer to the next question that naturally arises in pursuing this investigation, namely,—to what district, and to what age, does the most ancient Cymric literature, the body of poems attributed to Bards of the sixth century, really belong, and how does Arthur appear in them ? For it is evident that, if these poems are genuine, they must reflect the history of that period ; and hence, that their accordance with the ascertained distribution, and facts of the history of the Cymric race in the sixth century, must be taken as the test of the age commonly assigned to them. And "if we find that they do not re-echo to any extent the fictitious narrative of the events of the fifth and sixth centuries as represented in the Bruts, but rather the leading facts of the early history of the Cymry, as we have been able to deduce them from the older authorities, it will be a strong reason for concluding that they belong themselves to an earlier age." [5] Such are the grounds on which Mr. Skene proceeds in controverting the conclusions of that negative school of criticism represented by Mr. Stephens[6] and Mr. Nash,[7] and which was the natural reaction from the extravagances of the mythologic school of Owen Pughe, and Edward Williams, and, more particularly, of Davies,[8] and of Herbert.[9]

Mr. Skene thus states the result of his examination of these poems. First, as to the district of the ancient Cymric territory to which they belong : "Of a large proportion of the historical poems, the scenery and events lie in the north ; the warriors whose deeds they celebrate were 'Gwyr y Gogledd,' or Men of the North ; they are attributed to Bards (Merlin, Taliessin, Aneurin,

[5] *Four Ancient Books*, v. I. p. 225.   [6] *Literature of the Kymry.*
[7] *Taliessin, or the Bards and Druids of Britain.*
[8] *The Mythology of the British Druids.*
[9] *Britannia after the Romans,* and *The Neo-Druidic Heresy.*

and Llywarch Hen,) connected with the north; and are, in point
of fact, the literature of the Cymric inhabitants of Cumbria before
that kingdom was subjugated by the Saxon king,"[10] Edmund of
Wessex, and by him ceded to the Gaelic king, Malcolm, king of
Scots, in 946.   Secondly, as to the true age of these poems attributed to Bards of the sixth century, Mr. Skene, while considering
that the oldest of them may have their foundation in the national
lays of Bards, who lived amid the conflicts of contending races
in that century, does not "place these poems in their earliest consistent shape further back than the seventh century;" when "the
sudden rise of the Cymric population to power under Cadwallawn,
and the burst of national enthusiasm and excited hope, found vent
in poetry."[11]   Lastly, how do these earliest Cymric poems mention
Arthur, and where do they place him?   "Out of so large a body
of poems, there are only five which mention him at all, and then
it is the historical Arthur, the Guledig, to whom the defence of the
wall was entrusted, and who fights the twelve battles in the north,
and finally perishes at Camlan."[12]   And Mr. Skene very justly
advances this fact in confirmation of the high antiquity which,
controverting the conclusions of Mr. Stephens and Mr. Nash, he
assigns to these poems.   "If they occupied a place, as is supposed,
in Welsh literature, subsequent to the introduction of the Arthurian
Romances, we should expect these poems to be saturated with king
Arthur, his knights, and their adventures.   But it is not so."[13]
The fact is, on the contrary, as above-stated.   These results, therefore, of the critical examination of Cymric history, political and
literary, lead directly to the positive conclusion that the historical
Arthur having been a leader of the northern Cymry, the original
birthland of the Arthurian traditions was the region which now
forms Southern Scotland, and the English Border.

[10] *Four Ancient Books*, v. I. p. 242.   [11] Ibid. p. 243.
[12] Ibid. pp. 226-7.   [13] Ibid. p. 226.

SECTION (II).

Historical Conditions inimical to the Importation into the North of Arthurian Tradition.

But, for the sake of further assurance, let us suppose that the Arthurian traditions of Scotland did not originate there in an historical Arthur; and so, inquire whether the History of the Northern Cymry presents us with conditions favourable, or inimical, to the importation of such traditions, and their topographical preservation, if thus derived, and not original. What the general conditions are that favour, or oppose, the introduction of traditions and traditional topographies from countries in which they have had an actual basis in historical facts, I will not here venture to state. The defining of such conditions belongs, indeed, fundamentally, to a science not yet constituted, a Psychology, not of men considered individually, but collectively. Here it will be sufficient briefly to point-out the chief historical facts connected with the northern Cymry ; and then ask, whether there are, or not, in these facts, such conditions as our present historical, and psychological knowledge would make appear inimical to the derivation from Wales, or elsewhere, of the Arthurian traditional topography of Southern Scotland.

Of these facts, the first to be noted is, that the petty Cymric kingdoms of the north were finally absorbed in the greater kingdom, not only of a kindred Celtic race, but of a race with which the Cymry had never been, except temporarily or occasionally, at war; and a race, moreover, which had, like the Cymry themselves, been the champions of Christianity against Paganism during the whole of these now dim, but once passion-lit Pre-mediæval Centuries. The region which, in the tenth century, began to be known as Scotland[14] was, in the sixth century, after the withdrawal of the

[14] First so called in that part of the *Saxon Chronicle* composed about 975. *Scotia* is used first with its modern meaning by Marianus Scotus in the eleventh century.

Romans, occupied by the four nations, or rather tribes, of the
Cymry, the Scots, the Picts, and the Saxons; the three first, of
Celtic, the last, of Teutonic race. With the Picts on the north,
and the Saxons on the east, the Cymry were in constant warfare;
and had either the Saxons or the Picts finally succeeded in con-
solidating these various tribes in a new nationality, there would
be evident psychological grounds for the hypothesis that the
Arthurian traditions of Scotland were not the legendary records of
historical events which had there occurred, but of events which
had elsewhere happened, and of which the traditions had been
imported to console a conquered race under a foreign and hated
yoke. But neither by the Picts, nor by the Angles, with whom
they had been for centuries at war, were the Cymry of the north
finally absorbed; but by the Scots, a brother of whose king they
had themselves voluntarily elected to the throne in 918, previously
to their being regularly incorporated into the Scotish nationality
after the Treaty of 946, between Malcolm II. and their Saxon foe,
Edmund of Wessex.

But in these Pre-mediæval Centuries, ecclesiastical is even more
important than political history. The history of Christianity is
then, indeed, what the history of Philosophy and of Science has
become since the upbreak of the Catholico-feudal system of the
Mediæval Age; that which alone, making transparent the spirit
animating the outward forms of political changes, reveals to us their
deepest causes. For not only had Churchmen, in these ancient
centuries, a predominant influence in accomplishing, or retarding,
political revolutions; but with a native Church was indissolubly
connected the national language and literature. How, then, do
the chief facts of the ecclesiastical history of the northern Cymric
States bear on the question before us? Now we find that the
Christianity of Scotland was derived from two different sources.
Directly from Rome came the Missions to the Cymry and Angles

of the south; while those to the Scots and Picts of the north,
emanated from the Irish Church of St. Patrick. This latter Church
was distinctively monastic in its organization; and hence arose an
opposition between the two Christian Churches of North Britain,
which could not, in that Pre-mediæval Age, but have the most
important political, and other effects. For us, it is sufficient here to
note that it was the Irish, or Columban Church of the Scots that
ultimately acquired the supremacy; a supremacy marked by the
foundation, in the year 736, of the Church of S. Andrew; and
the general adoption of S. Andrew, instead of—as when the Church
of the Cymry (and Angles) had the ascendancy—S. Peter, as the
patron saint of the kingdom.[15] And hence we see that, in the
victory of the opponent Church with its Gælic language and literature, the way was already, in the eighth century, prepared, not only
for that political incorporation of the northern Cymric States in
the kingdom of the Scots which took place in the tenth century,
but for that complete absorption of the Cymric by the Gælic race,
indicated by such a speedy disappearance of the language of the
former that, at the opening of the Mediæval Age, in the eleventh
century, we find the various tribes of North Britain consolidated
into a Gælic-speaking kingdom.[16]

[15] Compare SKENE, *Chronicles of the Picts and Scots*, pp. clxx.-iv., INNES, *Sketches
of Early Scotish History*, ch. i. etc., and BURTON, *History of Scotland*, v. I. chs. vii.
and viii.

[16] " To account for the prevalence of a Teutonic speech throughout the southern
and eastern lowlands of Northern Scotland, the existence of a Teutonic people in this
quarter before the twelfth century is often vaguely assumed as a fact, without speci-
fying either their origin, or the time of their settlement. . . . . But if the main
body of the population of Scotland proper then spoke the Teutonic dialect which has
lasted till the present day, how is it to be explained that to speak *Scotice* in the twelfth
and thirteenth centuries was to talk *Gaelic?* If two distinct dialects of an origin so
different had existed beyond the Forth in the days of Huntingdon, how could he have
written about the extinction of the Pictish people and their language, when the
dialect which was not Scotish would have assuredly been regarded as Pictish? Above
all, Beda, who has left on record a Pictish word, unquestionably of *Celtic* origin, was
aware of no essential difference of race between the northern and southern Picts, or
indeed of any people of Teutonic origin in Britain, besides the Angles, Jutes, and

Still other facts there are, however, which seem to make incredible any other derivation of Scotish Arthurian topography than from an historical leader of the northern Cymry. For the conquering Scots were no illiterate horde of barbarians. On the contrary, " Anglo-saxon literature had not begun to spread when that of the Scots was supreme. . . . And by the Scots writers, whether of Dalriada or Ireland, the Saxons are spoken of without any affectation as barbarians, just as they would have been spoken of by the Romans. From the other side even, in Bede's own patriotic narrative, the sense of inferiority is distinctly apparent. Indeed he traces one of the greatest contributions towards their civilization which the Saxons received, directly to Iona."[17] And, what still more directly bears on the present question, the Scots had a traditional and poetic literature of their own, which must certainly have greatly opposed the introduction, after their incorporation of the Cymry, of Cymric poetry and tradition, and must, also, have been a condition highly unfavourable to the preservation of such tradition,

Saxons. . . . . . But did this Teutonic speaking colony arrive at a later period after the union of the Picts and Scots under the line of Kintyre ? If so, it must have been of Scandinavian origin. But history, which has preserved the remembrance of the Scandinavian settlements on the northern mainland, and throughout the western islands, is totally silent about any such colonization in the southern and eastern lowlands of ancient Alban. Where history is silent, topography sometimes reveals the secrets of the past. . . . . . But the map may be searched in vain for any such traces in the northern lowlands of a band of colonists so numerous and so important, as to retain this dialect, which they never stamped upon the face of the country, and to perpetuate it as one of the original sources of the Lowland Scotch spoken at the present day. The existence of such a population in such a quarter is as apocryphal as the mythical Scotish conquest. . . . The English wars stamped a nationality upon the descendants of the various races subject to the Rex Scotorum, and as the use of (Gaelic, and) Norman-French died away, and the ' quaint Inglis' of Southern Scotland and the civic population became the language of the king and his nobility, spreading gradually over the whole of those lowland districts which had long formed the heart of ancient *Alban*, the Gaelic tongue, rather than the Gaelic race, was at length confined to the mountains, and the names of *Scot* and *Scotland* were adopted as national and generic terms from the language which had now become the national speech. Henceforward to speak *Scotice* was to talk in the Lowland tongue."—ROBERTSON, *Scotland under Her Early Kings*, Appendix I. *Picts and Scots*, pp. 374-5 and p. 369.

[17] BURTON, *History of Scotland*, v. I. p. 332.

had it had, either before or after such incorporation, any other than a native, historical origin. But, to the third Chapter, in which I shall have to treat of the relation of the Fingalian to the Arthurian topography of Scotland, I shall defer any further notice of the Ossianic poetry of the Scots.

Suppose, then, that Y Gogledd, The North, or what we now call southern Scotland, was *not* the historical birthland of the Arthurian traditions, how came they there? Are there not, in the above stated facts, conditions in the highest degree inimical to the introduction of these traditions from without? Topographically rooted, popular traditions are phenomena that must have no slight causes. What causes do we find in the history of the North that are sufficient to explain its Arthurian topography, otherwise than as originating in the life and the wars of a native and historical Arthur? Mr. Pearson, indeed, maintains that the historical Arthur was sovereign of a territory in the southwest of England, of which Camelot or Cadbury, in Somersetshire was the capital; and, admitting how numerous are the Arthurian localities of Scotland, asks, "now assuming Arthur's history to become first extensively popular in the twelfth century, who are most likely to take it up, and identify it with localities in their own neighbourhood? The Saxons or Saxonized settlers in Devonia, or the Welsh and Picts of Galloway? Surely the latter. Which history can best be interpolated with strange facts? the history of the conquered and civilized western counties, or that of districts which long maintained their barbarous independence? Again, the latter."[18] But to this it appears sufficient to reply that the Cymry of the North were not only not in a state of "barbarous independence" in the twelfth century; but that, as above shown, they were unresistingly incorporated in the monarchy of the Scots in the tenth century; and that a Church and language opposed to their own had become supreme in Scotland in the eighth

---

[18] *Bishop Percy's Folio MS.*, v. I. p. 403.   See also Mr. Pearson's note, *infrà*, p. 133.

century.[19] If, therefore, Arthurian traditions are admitted to be thus numerous in Scotland, how can we account for their origin there on any reasonable hypothesis of importation?

In the fact, then, of the Pre-mediæval absorption of the northern Cymry by a kindred race, with whom they had never been at war; in the fact of the loss of their native language succeeding the subjection of their native church; and in the fact of the conquering Scots having a traditional and poetic literature of their own; there were conditions that seem to make it impossible to explain the existence of Arthurian localities in Scotland on any other theory than that to which we have been led by the critical examination of the earliest historical sources, and earliest bardic poems of the Cymry; namely, that these localities were, in the North, not the creations of a fond fancy acting on a transplanted tradition, but the genuine records of a native, historical hero.

SECTION (III).

Historical Conditions favourable to the Importation into the South of Arthurian Tradition.

Very different was the history of the Cymric kingdoms of what afterwards became the West of England, and the North-west of France. These, after a resistance, enduring with various fortune, for many centuries, were ultimately overpowered by a foreign, and chiefly Teutonic, race; against whom it was, and is, their pride to maintain their native language; and to preserve, or invent, glorifying traditions. Not here, as in the North, were the Cymry absorbed by a kindred race.

Further, not only were there migrations from Strathclyde and Cumbria, which would carry the Arthurian traditions, suppose them to have had their historical origin in the North, into new southern homes, but it was from the northern region of Manau, or Manann

---

[19] See also in answer to Mr. Pearson's objections to the theory maintained by Mr. Skene and myself, *infra*, p. 131.

that " Cunedda went with his sons, and gave a royal house to the
Throne of Wales, in the person of Maelgwn and his descendants.
And when this house failed in the person of Cynan Tyndathwy, there
is every reason to believe that the same region gave a second royal
house to Wales, in the person of Mervyn Frych ; " [20] and so, also, it
should seem that one dynasty, at least, of the kings of Cornwall was
descended from a northern family.   And that there were large and
frequent migrations from Cornwall to Brittany is well known.

And consider these critical results.   " If the poems attributed
to the bards of the sixth century really belong to that period,"
—(we have seen that, in Mr. Skene's opinion, they cannot be
carried further back in their earliest consistent shape, than the
seventh century)—"there is an interval of several centuries during
which such a literature either never existed, or has perished, till
the twelfth century, from which period a mass of poetic literature
existed in Wales, and has been preserved to us.   Of the genuine
character of that poetry there seems to be no doubt." [21]   As to the
Cymric literature of Brittany, the *Poemes des Bards Bretons au
Sixième Siècle*, of M. de la Villemarqué, can only for a moment mislead
by its title.   It is, in fact, but a French edition of those ancient Cymric
poems which, as we have seen, belong, in Mr. Skene's opinion,
to the northern kingdoms of Cumbria and Strathclyde, absorbed
by the Scotish nationality.   And considering how much the brilliant
volumes of M. de la Villemarqué have done in elucidating and popu-
larizing the whole cycle of Arthurian romance, it is with regret that
one finds grave suspicion cast on his perfect honesty as a collector of
Breton ballads ; and objections, hitherto, I believe, unanswered
raised against the genuineness of what have been given to the world
as ancient Cymric poems of Brittany.   But this being so, we are left
with the Four Ancient Books of *Wales*, or rather, if Mr. Skene's
criticism of them is accepted, of *Arthurian Scotland*, as presenting to

[20] *Four Ancient Books*, v. I. pp. 93-4.   [21] Ibid. p. 19.

us the only genuine fragments of Cymric literature of the Pre-mediæval Age.

Remark also the fact that it was with the loss of national independence that all the genuine Cymric literature, later than these Four Books, arose. With the defeat and death of Rhys ap Tewdwr, fighting against the Normans under Robert Fitzhamon, the kingdom of South Wales came to an end in 1090. And though native princes still ruled in North Wales till 1282, the death in that year of Llywelyn was followed by the subjugation of all Wales by King Edward the First. It was cotemporaneously with these events that Welsh literature arose, and that the MSS. were written which we now possess of the ancient poems of the northern Cymry, by this time completely absorbed in the new nationality to which the conquering Celtic race of the Scots had given their name. In a literature composed under such circumstances, it is evident that the localization of Arthur in Wales [22] can be of no independent force; nor can it, indeed, be regarded as anything more than such a localizing and magnifying of northern Cymric traditions, as was calculated to soothe a conquered race in their dejection, and to flatter them with new hope.

And, finally, observe that, throughout the whole of this southern region, the ground was most eminently prepared for the reception of Arthurian traditions. For, in the first place, there must, by the eleventh or twelfth centuries, have been many traditions of conquest, as of defeat, during the half-millenium of wars with the Saxons. There may, also, during these five hundred years, very probably have been southern leaders of the same name as the great northern Guledig of the sixth century; or leaders, such as Dr. Guest's Owen Finddu (?) (above p. 11, n. 21) whose story

---

[22] Nor even, when Arthur is placed by this later literature in Wales, does this necessarily mean the present Principality; for by writers of this age—Froissart for instance—the mountains of *Cumberland* were still called *Wales.*

could readily get confounded with that of Arthur. And, further, though the traditions of Arthur, Guenivere, and Lancelot, of Merlin the Bard, of Perceval, Gawayne, and Mordred, would appear to have had their historical origin among the Northern Cymry of what is now Southern Scotland; yet these, though the main, are not the only traditions on which the Arthurian Romance-cycle is founded; and Wales, Cornwall, and Brittany very possibly had the way prepared for the introduction from the North of the main Arthurian tradition, by the existence in each of them already of traditions with which the northern story might be readily connected. As to what, how-ever, really were the native Arthurian traditions of Wales, Corn-wall, and Brittany respectively, I will not here venture to say more than that the tradition of Mark should seem to be the special con-tribution of Cornwall to the cycle of Arthurian romance. How similar the story of Mark is to the *domestic* tradition of Arthur need hardly be noted; except more clearly to show how readily explicable, on the theory here maintained, is the association in Cornish localities of the traditions of Mark and of Arthur.

Considering these facts—the conquest by a foreign race, but pre-servation of the language, of the Cymric kingdoms of the South; the Cymric migrations from, but not to, the North, and the northern descents of some of the southern dynasties; the Mediæval, and not Pre-mediæval, age of the whole of Cymric literature, except those earlier poems in which Arthur is but some half-dozen times men-tioned, and then, as it should seem, as a leader of the Northern Cymry; the upburst of this Mediæval Cymric literature cotempo-raneously with the last struggles for, and final loss of, national in-dependence; and the general preparation of the southern kingdoms for the transplanting of Arthurian localities;—can we refuse to see conditions in the highest degree favourable to the importation from the North of the Arthurian traditions of the West of England and the North-west of France?

Such, then, are the theoretical considerations, arising from the latest results of the criticism of Cymric history and literature ; considerations that lead us both directly, and indirectly, to the conclusion that Southern Scotland and the English Border was the historical birthland of the main Arthurian traditions. For, not only does the direct criticism of the earliest historical records, and earliest bardic poems, lead to the conclusion that Arthur was an actual sixth-century leader of the northern Cymry ; but the further investigation of Cymric history presents to us conditions highly unfavourable in the North, and highly favourable in the South, to an hypothesis of the outward derivation of the Arthurian traditions of which, both in the North and in the South, we find topographical records.   But, as I have above admitted, the materials for forming an assured critical conclusion on such a question as the present are too scanty, to make our theory independent of verification from some other line of research.   How is this to be attempted ?   By a thorough investigation of the Arthurian topography of the North.   For if we should find that Arthurian localities are here more numerous than in any of the other regions of the Old Arthurland ; that these localities are not spread over Scotland, but are confined to the region which in the sixth, but not after the tenth century, was mainly peopled by a Welsh-speaking race ; that they are thickest just where the battles between the Cymry and their Saxon and Pictish foes must have been most frequent ; that the exceptions to the rule of Arthurian localities being found only where there was anciently a Cymric population, do but make the accordance between tradition and historical fact all the more striking ; and that, finally, with localities in the North, not Arthur only, but all the chief characters of Arthurian Romance, are connected ; I think it will have to be conceded that we have a very complete inductive verification of our theoretical conclusions from the criticism of Cymric History.

CHAPTER III.

THE CHIEF COUNTRY OF ARTHURIAN LOCALITIES, AS GENERALIZED FROM AN EXPLORATION OF SOUTHERN SCOTLAND AND THE ENGLISH BORDER.

LET me now proceed to give the generalized result of my exploration of the existing Arthurian Topography of the region indicated by the criticism of Cymric history as the birthland of Arthurian tradition, in a narrative of a single hypothetical journey in which a very great number of actual journeys through particular districts are connected, as in the route on the accompanying map. Let us suppose ourselves, then, to start from the Braes of Mar, at the foot of Ben-Muich-Dhui,[1] the central dome of that mountain range of the Grampians, which, as we shall find in the next chapter, separates Arthurian, from Fingalian Scotland. For, journeying, and it must be on foot, up Glen Cluny, and Glen Callater;—ascending the wild, and solitary heights at the head of Loch Callater to the plateau of the Kinlochan Forest;—passing along the eastern edge of the deep glen which runs up through this plateau, with hawks and eagles over head, and great herds of red deer in the woody pastures of the glen below;—and travelling through Upper and Lower Glen Isla; we shall, in a single day's journey,—but of some thirty or forty miles,—pass through scenery which will remain in our recollection as a grand background to that of Arthurian Scotland; and, coming down on the most north-eastern group of Arthurian localities, our route will be southwards, through the eastern part of the Arthurian region, and then up again, northwards, on its western side.

We shall thus explore successively three great divisions of Arthu-

---

[1] For a more detailed account of this grand central district of Scotland than is found in the ordinary Guide-Books, see BURTON'S *Cairngorm Mountains*, and TAYLOR'S *Braemar Highlands*; the former, for mountain climbing; and the latter, for traditional tales.

rian localities—an Eastern, a Southern, or Border, and a Western
Division; and the very numerous localities of each of these divisions we shall find to lie in three naturally distinguished districts,
giving us, thus, in "the North," no less than nine distinct Districts
of Arthurian Localities. And, further, we shall find these localities
to be of three different classes, which may be distinguished as Traditional, Historical, and Poetical; the first, being localities which, in
their names and the still living traditions attached to them, are
Arthurian; the second, being identifications of places connected with
the Arthurian story as it is found in the earliest historical sources;
and the third, being identifications of places mentioned in those Four
Ancient Books of Cymric Poetry which we have found to belong, in
their subject-matter, to the Arthurian Age, meaning by that term,
not merely the generation of Arthur, but the century which opens
with his exploits. That, side by side with these identifications of
historical and poetical sites, we should find a very great number
of traditional localities, is evidently, in itself, and apart from other
considerations, no slight proof of the correctness of these identifications.

SECTION (I).

The Eastern Division of Arthurian Scotland.

Lower Glen Isla lies between the main line of the Grampians
and the lower range of hills, through the eastern end of which the
road passes. Here we find ourselves with a wooded hill on the
right, and, on the left, a steep, furze-covered hill, the last of the
range in this direction, and with the remains of what has apparently
been a formidable stronghold on its summit. It is Barry-hill (*Barra*,
fortified hill), and the first Arthurian locality of what I would distinguish as *District I.—Strathmore.* I ascend its grassy sides, crossed
by many a sheep-track, and am sorry its rabbit-inhabitants disturb
themselves so much to get out of my way. Seated on the higher of

the two lines of entrenchment, and looking down on the great valley of Strathmore, stretching across to the seaward range of the Sidlaw Hills, and with the Isla winding through it, past the "bonnie house o' Airlie," I recall its Arthurian traditions. For innumerable legends agree in representing it as the Castle to which the Pictish king Mordred, having defeated King Arthur in a great battle, carried off as a prisoner his queen Quenivere, or, as she is locally named, Ganora, Vanora, or Wander.[2] This, however, it seems, she found by no means so unpleasant as she ought to have done. For "Vanora," says tradition, "held an unlawful intercourse with Mordred; and Arthur, when he received her again," did not act with the magnanimity of Mr. Tennyson's *flos regum*, but, "enraged at her infidelity, caused her to be torn to pieces by wild horses."[3] As an old fellow, however, with whom I got into talk on the road near this, and who told me a legend I had not previously heard of the four places in this neighbourhood where the parts of Queen Vanora's dismembered body were buried, sagely remarked: "Thae auld histories are maistly lees, I'm thinkin'."

Her tomb (or principal tomb), "Ganore's Grave," lies but a few miles off. For "she was buried at Meigle, and a monument erected to perpetuate her infamy." Gray, who visited the place from Glammis Castle, notes: "Passed through Meigill, where is the tomb of Queen Wander, that was riven to death by stoned horses for nae gude that she did,—so the woman here told me, I assure you."[4] And on examining the curious sculptured stones in Meigle churchyard,[5] said to be the remains of this monument, we do actually find "two representations of wild beasts tearing a human body,—and one where the body seems tied, or close to chariot

---

[2] Called Wanore and Vanore in the Scotish Romance of *Lancelot of the Laik* of 1478 or 1490. See pp. 230 and 575. Edit. E.E.T. Soc.
[3] *New Statistical Account of Scotland*, v. X. 118.
[4] *Works* (1825) v. II. p. 274.
[5] See STUART's *Sculptured Stones of Scotland*.

wheels,—which may relate to Vanora, or may have given rise to
the tradition."[6] This is otherwise described by Archdeacon Sinclair,
of Glasgow, in a MS. of the year 1560, as, "Ane goddess in ane caert
and twa hors drawand her."[7] But the scene of her last resting place,
when I visited it, seemed suggestive of some less rude, some nobler
version of her story. It was the close of autumn. Along the
broad valley of Strathmore, ending northwards in the Howe of the
Mearns, and sheltered from the sea by the Sidlaw Hills, with their
many legends of Duncan, Macbeth,[8] and Banquo, the farm-yards
were closely stacked with the ingathered corn; the leaves, whirled
by gentle breezes, were falling through the sunny air; and beneath
the lofty range of the snow-capped Grampians, lay the dying year
in the beauty of an ineffable repose.

Mordred thus appears, in Scotish tradition, as both the political
hostis, or foe, and the domestic *inimicus*, or unfriend, of Arthur; but
in Mediæval Romance he commonly occupies the former position
only, while his traditional part, as the lover of Guenivere, is taken
by Lancelot. The question then arises, can Lancelot, as well as
Mordred, be localized in Scotland? Now M. de la Villemarqué
very ingeniously identifies Lancelot, or L'Ancelot, with the Cymric
chieftain Mael: "Les plus anciens manuscrits . . . . portent souvent
Ancelot . . . . *Ancel*, en langue romane, signifie *servant*, et Ancelot
est son diminutif . . . . Si, par hasard, Ancelot était la traduction
du nom d'un personnage gallois, dont l'histoire s'accorderait en tout
point avec le roman? Eh bien, c'est ce que je crois avoir découvert
on trouve, en effet dans les traditions celtiques, un chef dont le nom

<hr>

[6] *New Stat. Ac.* v. X. p. 234.

[7] Quoted by CHALMERS (of Auldbar) *Sculptured Stones of Angus and Mearns.*

[8] It would hardly be fair to Shakspeare's hero to omit noting that, in the general
rehabilitation of traditional villains, which modern historians have done so much to
accomplish, Macbeth has been found one of the greatest of Scotland's kings.—
ROBERTSON, *Scotland under Her Early Kings*, v. I. p. 121–4. BURTON, *History of
Scotland*, v. I. p. 370-7.

Mael (serviteur) répond exactement à celui *d'Ancelot*, et à qui les anciens bardes, les triades, les chroniques, les legends, et toutes les autorités armoricanies, galloises on étrangeres prêtent les mêmes traits, le même caractère, les mêmes mœurs, les mêmes aventures qu'au héros du roman français."[9]   And, if we accept this identification, then Lancelot, as well as Mordred, belongs to Scotland.   For " le chef Mael, selon les bardes gallois, avait dans l'Ecosse des domaines où il la mena."[10]   But we may far more directly identify the country of Lancelot with a Scotish district, for he is uniformly spoken of in the Romances as the son of " le roy Ban de Benoic ; " and in the Scotish *Lancelot* of 1478, this " Benoic" is at once identified for us in the lines—

> " a knycht clepit Lancelot of ye Laik,
> That sone of Bane was king of Albanak "—[11]

Albanak, or Alban, being the well-known name applied to Scotland beyond the Firths of Forth and Clyde.[12]   And that it was in the eastern part of that region that the kingdom of Lancelot's father was situated, we may presume from the fact of its having been "le roy Claudas de la terre d'Escosse" (the western kingdom of the Scots of Dalriada ?) who "mena guerre contre le roy Ban de Benoic et le roy Boort de Ganues (or Gannes) tant quil les desherita de leurs terres."[13]   Thus, the Mael of tradition, and the Lancelot of romance, and the Mordred both of tradition and romance, are as closely connected in the scenes, as in the stories of their lives.

In very remarkable proximity to the Castle of Mordred, and the Grave of Guenivere, we find near Meigle, and in the parish of Cupar Angus, a standing stone called the Stone of Arthur ; near it, again,

---

[9] *Les Romans de la Table Ronde*, pp. 58-9.
[10] Ibid. p. 64, citing *The Myryrian Archæology*, v. I. p. 175.
[11] Lines 201-2, p. 7, of the Edition of the E. E. Text Soc.
[12] *Book of the Dean of Lismore*, p. lxxv.
[13] *Lancelot du Lac*, f. 1.

a gentleman's seat, called Arthur's Stone; and not far from it a farm called Arthur's Fold.[14] And "a rock on the north side of the hill of Dunbarrow, in Dunnichen parish (in the adjoining county of Forfar), has long borne, in the tradition of the country, the distinguished name of Arthur's Seat."[15] This parish, it may be noted, is further remarkable as the scene of that great defeat of the Saxon Ecfrid, in 680, which permanently secured the country between the Tay and the Forth from the influences that would have made it part of England.[16]

And the Tay,—of which the old name was Tava, from the Gaelic *Tamh*, smooth, of which *Taw* is the Cymric equivalent,—is more than once mentioned in the *Four Ancient Books*, as, for instance, in the *Black Book of Caermarthen:*

> "It is not the nearest Tawy I speak of to thee,
> But the furthest Tawy."[17]

And the Scotish Tay, and not the river of that name in South Wales, seems to be also alluded to in the Dialogue between Merlin and his sister Ganieda in the *Red Book of Hergest:*

> "Rydderch Hael, the feller of the foe,
> Dealt his stabs among them,
> On the day of bliss at the ford of Tawy."[18]

Between Perth on the Tay, and Stirling on the Forth, we find no Arthurian localities. But at the latter river, we enter on *District II.—Firth of Forth.* The banks of the Forth should seem to have been the scene of a dispute as to who should lead in crossing the river, of which a curious legend is preserved in the Venedotian code of the *Old Welsh Laws* (p. 50).[19] And on

---

[14] *New Stat. Ac.*, v. I. p. 506. Pennant, *Second Tour in Scotland*, v. II. pp. 177–8. Bellenden's Boece, fo. lxviii.

[15] *New Stat. Ac.*, v. I. p. 419.

[16] Burton, *History of Scotland*, v. I. p. 313.

[17] *Four Ancient Books*, v. I. p. 294.

[18] Ibid. p. 463.

[19] Ibid. v. I. pp. 174-5.

the Links of Forth, Mr. Skene would find the site of Arthur's
tenth battle, "in litore fluminis quod vocatur Treuruit." "There
is much variety in the readings of this name, other MSS. reading it 'Trath truiroit;' but the original Cymric form is given
us in two of the poems in the *Black Book;* it is in one *Try-
wruid,* and in the other *Tratheu Trywruid.* There is no known
river bearing a name approaching to this. *Tratheu,* or shores,
implies a sea-shore or sandy beach, and can only be applicable
to a river having an estuary. An old description of Scotland,
written in 1165 by one familiar with Welsh names, says that
the river which divides the 'regna Anglorum et Scottorum et
currit juxta oppidum de Strivelin' was 'Scottice vocata *Froch,*
Britannice *Werid.*' [20] This Welsh name for the Forth at Stirling
has disappeared, but it closely resembles the last part of Nennius'
name, and the difference between *wruid,* the last part of Nennius'
name Try-wruid, and Werid is trifling. The original form must have
been Gwruid or Gwerid, the G disappearing in combination." [21] So
far Mr. Skene. And it must be, at least, remarked that not only
has no more probable site been found for this tenth battle, but that
we have a strong confirmation of the above argument in favour of
the Links of Forth, in the fact of Stirling being undoubtedly a
traditional Arthurian locality.

For William of Worcester tells us that "Rex Arturus custo-
diebat le round table in Castro de Styrlyng, aliter Snowden West
Castell." [22] And Snowdon, which is also the official title of one of
the Scotish heralds, has no connection with the Welsh mountain of

---

[20] *Chronicle of the Picts and Scots,* p. 136. "It may seem strange," says Mr.
Skene, "that I should assert that Gwryd and Forth are the same word. But *Gwor* in
Welsh is represented by *Fear* in Irish, the old form of which was *For,* and final *d* in
Welsh is in Irish *ch,* in Pictish *th.* The river which falls into the Dee, near Bala,
in North Wales, is called Try-weryn, a very similar combination."

[21] *Four Ancient Books,* v. II. pp. 56-7.

[22] *Itinerary,* p. 311.

that name, but is simply the descriptive name of Stirling—Snua-dun, the fort, or fortified hill, on the river.[23]

> " Stirling's tower
> Of yore the name of Snowdoun claims,"

says Sir Walter Scott,[24] and, in a note, quotes Sir David Lindsay :

> " Adew, fair Snawdoun, with thy towris hie,
> Thy Chapell-royall, park, and *Tabyll Round :*
> May, June, and July would I dwell in thee,
> Were I a man, to hear the birdis sound,
> Whilk doth agane thy royal rock rebound." [25]

The Table Rounde here mentioned, and which I found to be now more generally known as the King's Knot, is a singular flat-surfaced mound within a series of enclosing embankments, which would appear to be of very great antiquity; and where, "in a sport called 'Knights of the Round Table,' the Institutions of King Arthur were commemorated," [26] at least, to the close of the Mediæval Age. How current, in Scotland, were Arthurian tales in the fourteenth and fifteenth centuries is witnessed-to by the poet I have just quoted, who, in his *Dreme*, speaks of having diverted James V. when young, " with antique storeis, and deidis martiall,"

> " Of Hector, *Arthur*, and gentile Julius,
> Of Alexander, and worthy Pompeius."

But, indeed, such evidence is unnecessary, considering that we still possess Scotish Arthurian Romances of that period.[27]

Near Larbert, and not far from where are now the Carron Ironworks, is, or rather was,—for it was destroyed many years ago by its barbarian proprietor,—what would appear to have been a Roman structure, but which, since the thirteenth century, at least, had been known as Arthur's O'on (Oven). For in 1293, in the reign of

---

[23] CHALMERS, *Caledonia*, v. I. p. 245.

[24] *Lady of the Lake*, Canto VI. S. xxviii.   [25] *Complaynt of the Papingo*.

[26] *New Stat. Ac.*, v. VIII. p. 407, citing WILLIAM OF WORCESTER, BARBOUR, GOUGH'S, CAMDEN'S *Britannia*, and CHALMERS, *Caledonia*, v. I. p. 244–5.

[27] See IRVING, *History of Scotish Poetry*, Chs. II. and III. But his account of these Scotish Romances is incomplete.

Alexander III., William Gourley granted to the monks of Newbotle "firmationem unius stagni ad opus molendini sui del Stanhus
quod juxta *Furnum Arthuri*, infra Baronium de Dunypas est." [28]

Proceeding up the Carron, which even Mr. Pearson identifies with
the Carun Fluvius of Nennius,[29] we are struck with the appearance of
two very singular conical hills, or mounds, in the park of Dunipace
House. These Mr. Skene would make the site of Arthur's sixth
battle "super flumen quod vocatur Bassas." [30] There is now no
river of this name in Scotland; but, as Mr. Skene remarks, "the
name Bass is also applied to a peculiar mound having the appearance of being artificial, which is formed near a river, though really
formed by natural causes. There is one on the Ury river in
Aberdeenshire, termed the Bass of Inverury, and there are two
on the bank of the Carron, now called Dunipace, erroneously supposed to be formed from the Gaelic and Latin words *Duni pacis*,
or hills of peace, but the old form of which was *Dunipais*, the latter
syllable being no doubt the same word Bass. Directly opposite, the
river Bonny flows into the Carron, and on this river I am disposed
to place the sixth battle." [31]

But I venture to think that a personal inspection of the ground
would not only have convinced Mr. Skene that the Park of Dunipace was a very unlikely place for a great battle, but have shown
him, on the opposite side of the Carron, almost directly opposite
these mounds, and in the angle formed by the junction of the
Bonny with the Carron, another, and vastly larger Bass; a moraine (?)
with three of its sides (those towards the Bonny and Carron)
as steep and sharply defined at the edges as walls, and forming
a natural stronghold, the broad flat summit of which, waving—

---

[28] *Charta Newbotle*, No. 239, cited by CHALMERS, *Caledonia*, v. I. p. 245.

[29] *Historical Maps—Britannia Cambrica*.

[30] "The printed text of the Vatican MS. of Nennius has *Lussas*, but this is a mistake, the original MS. reads Bassas."—SKENE'S note.

[31] *Four Ancient Books*, v. I. pp. 53–4.

when I scaled it from the river side—in acres of clover, would scarce need defence except in the rear, where it slopes gradually to the south.   This natural fortress must certainly have been the scene of many a conflict between Cymry, Picts and Saxons in the Arthurian Age; and all Mr. Skene's arguments would, as it appears to me, apply with ten-fold more force to this Bass than to those he has fixed on, as the site of the sixth battle of the Arthur of Nennius. From an old man, with whom I had some talk on the Bridge of Carron, I found that, in spaets, the river not unfrequently overflowed to the very base of this hill, and that it, and the farm to which it belongs, is called Roughmute.   And many a rough moot, or council, has no doubt been held there.

After the old man left me, I suddenly remembered, as I looked over the bridge, and up the river, that the Carron was one of Ossian's favourite streams.

"I behold not the form of my son at Carun; nor the figure of Oscar in Crona. The rustling winds have carried him far away, and the heart of his father is sad." [32]

And so, instead of proceeding on my way, I wandered up its southern banks for a mile or two, coming down to the bridge again on the other side.   Moraines, or whatever else they may be geologically, there is, on this southern bank, such a number of "Basses,"—of beautiful knolls, with woody dells, and shadowy braes,—such Fairy Highlands, as I do not remember to have elsewhere seen.   Well might the Doric Muse have been here inspired with these fine pastoral lines :—

> "O bonnie are the greensward howes,
>   Whar through the birks the burnie rowes,
>   An' the bee bums, an' the ox lowes,
>   An' saft winds rustle,
>   An' shepherd lads, on sunny knowes,
>   Blaw the blithe whustle."

Then, on again towards the scene of the final battle between Arthur and Mordred; having some talk on the way with a bridge-

[32] MACPHERSON, *The Poems of Ossian. The War of Caros.*

keeper whom I found beguiling the time with Brougham's "Discourse on the Study of Science." "However ignorant we may be," he modestly remarked, "we may benefit a little." Now, where is the site of the "Gweith Camlan in qua Arthur et Medraut coruere," to be more probably found than at the little town of Camelon where we now are? "It is surprising," says Mr. Skene, "that historians should have endeavoured to place this battle in the south, as the same traditions, which encircle it with so many fables, indicate very clearly who his antagonists were. Medraut or Modred was the son of that Llew to whom Arthur is said to have given Lothian, and who, as Lothus, king of the Picts, is invariably connected with this part of Scotland. His forces were Saxons, Picts, and Scots, the very races Arthur is said to have conquered in his Scotish campaigns. If it is to be viewed as a real battle at all, it assumes the appearance of an insurrection of the conquered districts, under Medraut, the son of that Llew to whom one of them was given."[33] Remark, further, not only that the site bears still the very same name as the battle; but that it is, as we have already in part seen, in the centre of a group of Arthurian localities; and further that, as history has shown, it is well fitted to be a great battle-field. For, in later historical times, two great battles have been fought at, or near Camelon; that of Falkirk, but a mile distant, in 1298, between the Scots and the English; and that of Falkirk-muir, in 1746, between the Hanoverian forces, under General Hawley, and the Highlanders, commanded by Prince Charles Stuart.

But twenty-one years before this final Arthurian battle of the year 537, namely, in 516, was fought that twelfth battle "in Monte Badonis," of Nennius, the "obsessio Montis Badonici," of Gildas, the site of which has given rise to so much discussion. "It has been supposed to have been near Bath, but the resemblance of names seems alone to have led to this tradition. Tradition equally

---

[33] *Four Ancient Books*, v. I., pp. 59-60.

points to the northern Saxons as the opponents, and in Ossa Cylel-laur,[34] who is always named as Arthur's antagonist, there is no doubt that a leader of Octa and Ebissa's Saxons is intended ; while at this date no conflict between the Britons and the West Saxons could have taken place so far west as Bath. The scene of the battle near Bath was said to be on the Avon, which Layamon[35] mentions as flowing past Badon Hill. But on the Avon, not far from Linlithgow, is a very remark-able hill, of considerable size, the top of which is strongly fortified with double ramparts, and past which the Avon flows. This hill is called Bouden Hill. Sibbald says, in his *Account of Linlithgowshire*, in 1710, 'On the Buden Hill are to be seen the vestiges of an outer and inner camp. There is a great cairn of stones upon Lochcote Hills, over against Buden, and in the adjacent ground there have been found chests of stones, with bones in them, but it is uncertain when or with whom the fight was.' As this battle was the last of twelve which seem to have formed one series of campaigns, I venture," says Mr. Skene, "to identify Bouden Hill with the Mons Badonicus." [36]

After enjoying the beautiful view from the top, with the Little Bouden and Cockleroy Hills on my right, as I looked north over the undulating country about Linlithgow, with its ancient royal palace on the lake, across to the fine estuary of the Forth, the shores of Fife and Clackmannan, and the Ochil Hills (Sliabnochel, or Ocelli Montes) ; I found, in talk with an old man of upwards of fourscore ("81 on the 21st of last July"), who was breaking stones on the roadside, what appeared to me an interesting confirmation of Mr. Skene's hypothesis, in a tradition of Arthur's presence here, at least,

---

[34] May there not be a reminiscence of this name in the Gallehault of the French, and the Galyot of the Scotish, Romance of *Lancelot ?*

[35] " There sank to the bottom five and twenty hundred, so that all Avon's stream was bridged with steel."—*Brut.* Edit. MADDEN, v. II. p. 469.

[36] *Four Ancient Books*, v. I. pp. 57–8.

if not also, of an Arthurian siege of Bouden Hill. After pointing out to me the "Fechtin' Fuird," about three-quarters of a mile below Bouden Hill, "from which they say that the Romans lifted their camp to gang to besiege Jerooslem;"[37] and telling me that on Cockleroy there was "a bit hollow on the tap, whaur twa or three men micht lie, ca'd the Bed o' Wallace;" I asked him how the hill got so curious a name? "Ou," said he, chuckling, and taking a pinch from his snuff-mull, "They say it was because the king was cockled (cuckolded) there." "What king?" said I, "any of the Stuarts?" "Na, I never heard it was ony o' the Stuarts at the pailace doon by; but it's mentioned in history[38] that King Arthur's wife was na' faithfu', an maybe it was her that was ouer cosh (too intimate) wi' anither man on the tap there."

Then, on to Linlithgow, which appears in Mr. Pearson's *Index*[39] as the Llechlleuteu of Aneurin, and thence down, some three miles, to the shore of the Firth and Caredin.

> "Let the Caer of Eiddyn deplore
> The dread and illustrious men clothed in splendid blue."[40]

For this, as it would appear, was the site of the conflict which is the subject of the first part of that great poem of the "Gododin" which

---

[37] Would it be too much to consider this legend of a camp under Bouden as a memory of the Arthurian Obsessio Montis Badonici which had got attributed to the Romans; and this particularly, as there are many legends of Arthur's having gone to Jerusalem; as there is no considerable historical improbability in his actually having done so; and as, if he made an Eastern pilgrimage, it would probably have been after this twelfth victory, which gave the kingdom peace till the fatal battle of Camlan, in which Arthur fell, twenty-one years later. Very probably, had I asked the old man whether he did not mean that it was Arthur, and not the Romans, who "lifted" the camp, he would have assented. But one cannot get truth if one does not guard against the temptation to put such leading questions in support of one's theories.

[38] I found that such phrases as "auld histories," and "mentioned in history," did not mean, with these old men, written, but traditional history.

[39] *Historical Maps—Britannia Cambria.*

[40] *Four Ancient Books,* v. I. p. 413 and v. II. p. 394. See also v. I. p. 378 and v. II. p. 374.

"has attracted so much attention, from its striking character, its apparent historic value, and the general impression that, of all the poems, it has the greatest claims to be considered the genuine work of the (Arthurian) bard (Aneurin) in whose name it appears." [41] After criticising the various theories, as to the site of this conflict, which have been put forward by Mr. Williams, M. de la Ville- marqué, Mr. Stephens, Mr. Nash, and Mr. Vere Irving, Mr. Skene thus proceeds :—

"It is plain from the poem that two districts, called respectively Gododin and Catraeth, met at or near a great rampart; that both were washed by the sea; and that in connection with the latter was a fort called 'Eyddin'. . . . . . . The name of Eyddin takes us at once to Lothian, where we have Dunedin or Edinburgh, and Caredin on the shore, called by Gildas 'antiquissima civitas Britonum.' That the Edin in (the former of?) these two names is the Eyddin of the poem is clear from a poem in the *Black Book of Caermarthen*, where Edinburgh is called Mynyd Eiddin;" and in a poem in the *Book of Taliessin* there is the expresion "Rhuing Dineiddyn ac Dineiddwg," where Dineiddyn can hardly be anything but Dunedin. At Caredin the Roman wall terminated. . . . . And Caredin is not far from the river Avon, and parallel to it flows the river Carron, the two rivers enclosing a district at the west end of which is a great moor still called Slamannan; in old Gaelic "Sliabh Manand," the moor or plain of Manand. This is the "Campus Manand" of Tighernac, and the Avon and Carron are meant by the Haefe and Caere of the *Saxon Chronicle*, and the Heue and Cere of *Henry of Huntingdon*. Now Gododin contained this district. For the *Guotodin* of the "Manau Guotodin," mentioned by Nennius as "regio in sinistrali parte insulæ" (an expression equivalent in Welsh to 'y gogledd,' or the North), is plainly the same as the Gododin of Aneurin; and the Cymric *Manau* of Gododin is, in its Gaelic form, *Manand*. Gododin was,

[41] *Four Ancient Books,* v. II. p. 359.

therefore, equivalent to the north part of Lothian, and was washed by the Firth of Forth.[42] So much for the identification of Eyddin and Gododin. Now as to Catraeth. "The *Irish Annals* frequently mention a district called *Calathros*; as in *Tighernac* . . . . in 736, 'Bellum Cnuice Cairpre i Calathros uc etar linn du,' which latter place can be identified as Carriber on the Avon, near Linlithgow. Calathros, therefore, adjoined this district. Its Latin form was Calatria . . . . Now, in the address of Walter L'Espec at the battle of the Standard in 1130, as reported by Ailred . . . . Calatria is placed between Lothian and Scotland proper, north of the Firths. And Calatria is surely the Cymric Galtraeth,[43] which we know was the same place as Catraeth.[44] All the requirements of the site seem, therefore, satisfied in that part of Scotland where Lothian meets Stirlingshire, in the two districts of Gododin and Catraeth, both washed by the sea of the Firth of Forth; and where the great Roman Wall terminates at Caredin, or the fort of Eidin." [45]

"As to the date of the battle we are not without indications . . . . The combatants were, on the one side, the Britons and the Scots under Aidan; the enemy or 'Barbari' were the Pagan Saxons and the half-Pagan Picts of Manau Guotodin, called in the poem the 'bedin' or host of Gododin. And the identity of the battle of Catraeth with the 'bellum Miathorum' of Adomnan enables us to fix its date . . . . . . at 596. But the first part alone of the poem of the Gododin relates to this battle; the second part, or continuation, contains in it an allusion to the death

---

[42] This is also the opinion of Mr. Beale Poste; but Mr. Nash and Archdeacon Jones place Manau Guotodin in the district about Jedbugh, and extend it into Northumberland.

[43] For a further account of Calatria see *Chronicles of the Picts and Scots. Introduction*, p. lxxx.

[44] Catraeth is placed by Mr. Pearson "about Galashiels, or near Kelso, and not far from the Kale." *Historical Maps—Britannia Cambrica.* Compare also MADDEN, *Layamon's Brut.* v. III. p. 324.   [45] *Four Ancient Books,* v. II. p. 366-8.

of Dyfynwal Vrych, or Domnal Breck, which the bard (*not*
Aneurin) saw from the heights of Adoyn. The date of this event
is known to be in 542. The site is not difficult to fix. *Tighernac*
calls it Strathcauin ; the *Annals of Ulster*, Strathcairinn. The upper
part of the vale of the Carron, through which the river, after rising
in the Fintry Hills, flows, is called Strathcarron; but it also bore
the name of Strathcawin. . . . . . . And in the Statistical Account
of the parish of Fintry there is the following notice : 'At the foot
of the rock which encircles the western brow of the Fintry Hills
there is a considerable extent of table-land, and on the descent
below this starts out a knoll, *commonly known by the name of the Dun
or Down*, of a singular appearance. Its front is a perpendicular
rock, fifty feet high. The western extremity of this rock is one
solid mass.' This is surely the height of Adoyn." [46]   And having
here, at Caredin, viewed the site of the battle which is the subject
of that first part of the Gododin, composed by Aneurin, we shall, in
exploring the Lennox on our returning northern route, have an
opportunity of visiting the scene of the battle celebrated by the
later bard, who was the author of the second part of the poem.

I found that there had been recently discovered, near Caredin, a
stone with an inscription in admirable preservation, of the Second
Augustan Legion, on completing a certain distance of the wall
under Antoninus Pius. And near this, at the eastern end of the
wall, was that linguistically famous town "qui sermone Pictorum
Peanfahel, lingua autem Anglorum Peneltun appellatur," as Bede [47]
writes ; and as Nennius [48] names it, " Penguaul, quæ villa Scottice
Cenail . . . . dicitur." Passing through the dismally
dirty town of Burrowstowness, I turned up towards Linlithgow
again. While enjoying, towards the top of the steep ascent, the
splendour of the sunset over the river, and estuary of the Forth,

[46] *Four Ancient Books*, v. II. pp. 369–70. Compare also v. I. pp. 177–8.
[47] *Historia Ecclesiæ*, l. c.   [48] *Historia Britonum*, § 23.

the Frenessicum, or Frisicum Mare, (Frisian Sea) of Nennius;[49]
the Frisian Shore, where stood in the Arthurian Age that monastery
of Culross in which the young Kentigern was placed under the dis-
cipline of Sô. Servanus;[50] the sands on which, in a later age, Sir
Patrick Spens was walking when he received the king's (Alexander
III.) "braid letter,"—

> "To Noroway, to Noroway,
> To Noroway o'er the faem,
> The king's daughter to Noroway,
> It's thou maun tak her hame;"—

the royal Dunfermline in the Abbey of which, the chief Burial-
place of the kings of Scotland, is the tomb of Robert the Bruce;
and Loch Leven, with its romantic memories of Mary Queen
of Scots; a fine-looking fellow, but of unmistakeably English
aspect, came-up, with whom our common admiration of the glorious
scene drew me into conversation. Walking on with him, he invited me into his house to have a cup of tea; and I found that
he and his wife, a fair and hearty girl with a charming Northumbrian *burr*, one 'darrlin' in her arms, and another at her feet, as
she bustled about, were one of many English families of the artisan
class, now invited into, and peacefully settled in this district, where
their ancestors had had to maintain themselves by such hard fighting. Their happy looking home, kindness, and hospitality, could
not but bring into vivid contrast in my mind the present times, and
those we may hope they are preparing, with those of that Pre-
mediæval Arthurian age of which I had been thinking, and which
had been so truly described by my last road-side acquaintance, the
old stone-breaker of Bouden Hill, when he said, "I'm thinkin' that
in thae days,—aye, it 'll be mair nor a thoosan years ago,—there
were hereawa jist vawrious wild tribes a' fechtin thro' ither."

[49] For the Durham MS. adds " quod inter nos Scotosque est;" and Jocelyn (*Vita
Kentigerni*) terms the shore of Culross " Frisicum litus."

[50] As Kentigern's Life by Jocelyn in PINKERTON's *Vitæ Antiquissimorum Sanctorum* is very rare, I may refer to the compilation in BUTLER, *Lives of the Saints*,
v. I. p. 139.

Irongath Hill on the east side of the river Avon near Linlithgow appears to be the Agathes of the *Book of Taliessin*.[51] For the Avon is, in the *Gododin*, called the Aeron, and probably appears in the first part of the name " Iron." Sir R. Sibbald in his *History of Linlithgowshire* says "The tradition is current that there was a fight between the Romans and the natives under Argadus in this hill, and that it had its name from Argad;" which was the name of a son of Llywarch Hen.[52] Journeying to Edinburgh, we pass Dalmeny, which appears to be identifiable with the Caer Govannon of the Red Book of Hergest.[53] For in an old list of the churches of Linlithgow, printed by Reiner, appears " Vicaria de Qumanyn;" and Dalmeny was formerly called Dumanyn.[54] Abercorn on the Firth, where was anciently a famous monastery, is the Abercurnig of Gildas. Cramond or Caer Amond, which may be identified with Caer Vaudwy.[55]

> " Before Caer Vaudwy a host I saw
> Shields were shattered and ribs broken. [56]
>
> . . . .
>
> And when we went with Arthur of anxious memory
> Except seven, none returned from Caer Vaudwy." [57]

Caer Sidi of the *Book of Taliessin* [58] would appear to have been upon an island, and is, according to Mr. Skene, probably the Urbs Judeu of Nennius,[59] and Bede's island city of Giudi, which we may with great probability place on Inchkeith, in the Firth of Forth.[60] And between six or seven miles from Edinburgh we find the famous Catstane, the inscription on which Sir James Simpson reads as recording the grave of Vecta, the grandfather of Hengist and Horsa.[61]

At Edinburgh we find the site of Arthur's eleventh battle, which was fought " in monte qui dicitur Agned,"—that is, Mynyd Agned,

---

[51] *Four Ancient Books*, v. I. p. 337.   [52] Ibid. v. II. p. 401.
[53] Ibid. v. I. p. 287.   [54] Ibid. v. II. p. 452.   [55] Ibid. v. II. p. 411 and 352.
[56] Ibid. v. I. p. 294.   [57] Ibid. v. I. p. 265.   [58] Ibid. v. I. p. 276.
[59] The Judeu, however, of Nennius, Mr. Pearson places in the Jedburgh district.
[60] *Four Ancient Books*, v. II. p. 408.
[61] *On the Catstane, Kirkliston, etc.*, in *Proceedings of the Society of Antiquaries of Scotland*, v. IV. p. 119 *et seq.*

the Painted Mount, which seems to be clearly identified with Edinburgh, the southern stronghold of the Picts; [62] against whom, under
the name of *Cathbregion*, " contra illos que nos Cathbregyon appel-
lamus," and not against the Saxons, this eleventh battle would
appear to have been fought. And it may be noted that the words
which form the root of the epithets Cath Bregion and Brithwryr,
are, "*Brith*, forming in the feminine *Braith*, Diversicolor, Maculosus,
and *Brych*—the equivalent in Cymric of the Gaelic *Breac*—Macula.
Both refer to the name Picti, or painted : and Agned probably
comes from an obsolete word, *agneaw*, to paint, *agneaid*, painted." [63]
In a poem referring to Arthur the Guledig, in the *Black Book of
Caermarthen*, we read—

> " In Mynyd Eiddin
> He contended with Cynvyn
> By the hundred there they fell,
> There they fell by the hundred,
> Before the accomplished Bedwyr.
> On the strands of Trywruid," [64] etc.

Edinburgh, or rather its Castle, appears also under the name of
Castrum Puellarum, in the Charters, and of the Castle of Maidens,
and Dolorous Valley in the Romances. " Arthur's Seat," says
Chalmers, in a note to which he had been incited by the remark of
" a late inquirer," who had said that it was " a name of yesterday,"
" had that distinguished name before the publication of Camden's
Britannia in 1585, as we may see in p. 478 ; and before the publication of Major in 1521, as appears in fol. 28 ; and even before the
end of the 15th century, as Kennedy, in his flyting with Dunbar,
mentions *Arthur Sate* or ony Hicher Hill." [65]

Proceeding from Edinburgh towards Haddington, we may make
an excursion to Trapender, formerly Dunpender, and more anciently
Dunpeledur Law. Here is said to have been buried that Llew, or
Lothus, in whose establishment by Arthur, as a (tributary ?) king of

---

[62] MADDEN, *Layamon's Brut.* v. III. pp. 315–6.
[63] *Four Ancient Books*, v. I., p. 84.   [64] Ibid. v. I. p. 263 ; cf. also p. 276.
[65] *Caledonia*, v. I., p. 246 ; and RAMSAY's *Evergreen*, v. II., p. 65.

Lothian, the battle of Mynyd Agned seems to have resulted. On Dunpeledur also, as likewise on the three fortified rocks of Edinburgh, Stirling, and Dumbarton, at Dundonald, in Ayrshire, and Chilnacase, in Galloway, S. Monenna or Darerca of Kilslleibeculean, in Ulster, founded a church, and nunnery.[66] These foundations appear to synchronise with the re-establishment of the Christian Church in these districts by Arthur, who was pre-eminently a Christian hero fighting against pagan Saxons and apostate Picts. And it seems not improbable that Thenew, the daughter of King Lothus, was one of the virgins in the church in Dunpeledur. About the time of S. Monenna's death, however, in the year 518, this royal virgin had the misfortune to give birth to a fine boy, who afterwards became the apostolic missionary Kentigern, now more commonly remembered as S. Mungo.[67] And as her story of an immaculate conception did not meet with due credence among the barbarians; after an attempt to put her to death, in one legend on Dunpeledur (or Dunpender), in another on Kepduff, now Kilduff, she was cast adrift in a boat from Aberlady Bay.[68] And this romantic incident, putting us in mind of the similar story of Custaunce being sent adrift by the constable of Alla, King of Northumberland—

> " But in the same schip as he hire found,
> Hire and hire yonge sone, and all hire gere,
> He shulde put, and croude here fro the londe,
> And charge hire, that sche never eft come there.
> Hir litel child lay wepyng in hire arm,
> And in hire arme sche lulleth it ful faste,
> And unto heven hire eyghen up sche caste"—[69]

may be an inducement to visit the scene of it.

[66] Hence, perhaps, the name of *Castle of Maidens* applied to Edinburgh ?

[67] Mungu is translated by Jocelyn " Carus amicus." It is Welsh, and found thus: *Mwyn, clemens, urbanus, lenis.* Cu, in combination Gu, *Carus.* DAVIES, *Welsh Dictionary*.

[68] Compare *Four Ancient Books*, v. I. pp. 85–6, and the *Vita S. Kentigerni*, by JOCELYN in PINKERTON'S *Vitæ Antiquissimorum Sanctorum*.

[69] CHAUCER, *The Man of Lawe's Tale*.

In this district also, we must at least notice, if we do not think it worth while to visit, the sites which that writer in the *Gentleman's Magazine* of 1842, before mentioned,[70] fixed on as the probable scenes of Arthur's four battles on the Dubglas, or Duglas, and his sixth battle on the Bassas. The former battle he places on "the little river Dunglas, which has formed through successive ages the southern boundary of Lothian;" and, he continues, "When the Saxons were driven from their entrenchments on the Dunglas, their flight was directed" northwards; and, "forced again to face their foes beside the channel which separates the mainland from the remarkable isolated rock in the Frith of Forth, near the town of North Berwick, called the Bass, and which, by a trivial error, the historian designates 'the river Bassas,' the Saxons sustained a sixth defeat."[71] The battles on the Du(b)glas "in regione *Linnuis*" we shall, however, before the end of our journey, find, I think, to have been more probably situated on the Douglas in the *Lennox*, than here on the Dunglas in *Lothian*. And a more probable site of the battle on the Bassas we have, I venture to think, already found on the Bonny, at Dunipais (or Dunipaice). Finally, on our way into the next Arthurian district we shall pass on the borders of the counties of Edinburgh and Peebles, the Moss of Maw mentioned in the *Book of Taliessin* as the Bush of Maw.[72]

We enter now on the exploration of *District III.—Tweeddale.* —At Peebles on the Tweed, or Tywi of the *Four Ancient Books*,[73] we find one of the many wells, or fountains, dedicated to S. Mungo, the legend of whose birth we have just noticed. And we are here in the heart of the Nemus Caledonis whither Merlin is said, in the Latin *Vita Merlini*, to have fled after the battle of Arderyth, and where, according to the tradition re-

[70] Ch. I. p. xxxii.
[71] *Gentleman's Magazine*, v. XVII., N. S., 1842, p. 598.
[72] *Four Ancient Books*, v. I. p. 337, and v. II. p. 401.
[73] Vol. I. pp. 373, 432, 470 seq., 490 seq.; v. II. p. 337.

ported by Fordun,[74] he met Kentigern, and afterwards was slain
by the shepherds of Meldredus, a regulus of the country on the
banks of the Tweed, "prope oppidum Dunmeller." So, from the
Broughton station I set out on foot for Merlin's Grave at Drum-
melzier, in which the name of Meldredus is preserved, according to
Mr. Skene,[75] and that of Merlin according to M. de la Villemarqué.[76]

> " Questa è l'antiqua e memorabil grotta,
>   Ch'edificò Merlino, il savio Mago
>   Che forse ricordare odi tal' otta,
>   Dove ingannollo la Donna del Lago." [77]

Crossing to the south bank of the Tweed, and reaching the ancient
parish church and kirkton, or hamlet, by the Pausayl (*i.e.* Willow)
Burn, I was fortunate in making the acquaintance of the intelligent
shoemaker of the place. From his account there seemed to be some
doubt as to which of two localities here had the best traditional
right to be called the Grave of Merlin. That now certainly the
most picturesque, and maintained by the late Dr. Somerville, the
minister of the parish, to be the true site of the tomb, is by an
ancient thorn-tree, of which there is now a younger thriving offshoot (fair augury of a renewal of Merlin's fame), by the burnside,
a little above its junction with the Tweed, and at the foot of the
moraine, on which stands the kirk and manse. But it seems that,
at the corner of what is now a corn-field, there used to be a cairn,
called Merlin's Grave; and though the Pausayl does not at present
meet the Tweed at this spot, yet it did so for a time, in consequence
of a great spaet or overflow of the river, when the Scotish James
VI. became king of England, and so the prophecy was fulfilled that

> "When Tweed and Pausayl meet at Merlin's grave,
>   Scotland and England one king shall have." [78]

For me, not only the weight of authority, but the perennial

[74] *Scotichronicon*, B. III. C. xxvi.   [75] *Four Ancient Books*, v. I. p. 54.
[76] *Myrdhin, ou L'Enchanteur Merlin*, p. 3.
[77] Aʀɪosto, *Orlando Furioso*, C. ɪɪɪ. S. 10.
[78] See Cʜᴀᴍʙᴇʀs, *History of Peebleshire*, and Pᴇɴɴʏcuɪcᴋ, *History of Tweeddale*, p. 26.

thorn-tree decides the matter. For this is always introduced in
the romantic fictions that represent his ladye-love, Viviana,[79] as
imprisoning Merlin, not, in the earlier romances, at least, that
she might basely triumph over him, but that he might be with
her for evermore. And though, in its present disafforested state,
the scenery of the here narrow valley of the Tweed, and its
enclosing hills is somewhat disappointing; it cannot be looked on
with indifference by any one who knows how, "la plus ancienne
tradition romanesque a fait agir Merlin, comment elle a personnifié
et idéalisé en lui le dévouement passionné à tout ce que la grande
epoque chevaleresque jugeait digne de son respect; je veux dire la
religion, la patrie, la royauté, l'amour, l'amour pur, discret, délicat,
la solitude à deux éternellement enchanteé."[80] And well may the
French *savant* in his history of the bard, his works, and influence,
refuse to follow him,—" a travers les fantaisies des continuateurs et

---

[79] " It also seems evident," says the Rev. T. Price, " that it is to the Hwimleian,
or Chwifleian of Merlinus Silvestris," the historical Merlin of Scotland, " that we
are to attribute the origin of the Vivianc of the romances of Chivalry, and who acts
so conspicuous a part in those compositions, although it is true there is not much
resemblance betwixt the two names. But if we look into the poems of Merlin
Sylvestris, we shall find that the female personage of this name, which by the French
romances might easily be modified into Viviane, is repeatedly referred to by the bard
in his vaticinations. It also seems probable, as Chwifleian signifies a female who
appears and disappears, and also as the word bears some resemblance in sound to
Sybilla, that the bard, by a confusion of terms and ideas, not uncommon in early
writers, coined this name as an appellation for some imaginary character, and
thus furnished the original of Viviane." *Literary Remains*, v. I. p. 144. This
Merlin also had a twin-sister Gwendydd or Ganieda, who supplied her brother
with food, in his solitary wanderings in the Caledonian Forest. In a poem in
the *Red Book of Hergest* (*Four Ancient Books*, v. I. p. 462) she addresses him as
Llallogan or twin-brother. "And this," says Mr. Price, " will explain a passage
in the Life of S. Kentigern, in which it is said that there was at the court of
Rydderch Hael, a certain idiot named *Laloicen*, who uttered predictions:—' In
curia ejus quidam homo fatuus vocabulo Laloicen;' and in the *Scotichronicon* it is
stated that this Laloicen was *Myrddin Wyllt*. By connecting these several parti-
culars we find an air of truth cast over the history of this bard, as regards the
principal incident of his life, and there can be no reason to doubt that some of the
poetry attributed to him was actually his composition." *Literary Remains*, v. I.
p. 143. Cited *Four Ancient Books*, v. II. pp. 353 and 424.

[80] VILLEMARQUE, *Merlin*, p. 234.

des imitateurs de son noble panégyriste, Robert de Borron. L'esprit grivois et goguenard y remplace progressivement l'esprit moral et grave passé de la tradition bretonne dans l'œuvre francaise primitive. Le sentiment est chassé trop souvent par le rire; ce qui est élevé par ce qui est plat; le sérieux par l'amusant. A la fin, Merlin sera plus ou moins moulé sur le type scolastique et vulgaire du savant devenu fou d'orgueil, du sage Salomon que séduisent les femmes étrangères, du poëte Lucrèce que la perfide Lucile empoisonne, du vieillard de la comédie, victime de sa sotte passion. Et la verve de Rabelais, pas plus que l'art de Tennyson, ne parviendront complétement à vaincre la pitié qu' inspirera cette figure tombante."[81]

In the legends and romances of Merlin mention is ever made of a fountain, by which he used to meet his lady fair, and around which, as is the wont of love, he caused to spring up an enchanted Garden of Joy. Of no well, or fountain, however, could I hear either with the name, or a tradition, of Merlin attached to it. The sources, or wells of Tweed, though at an elevation of 1500 feet, lie in a hollow of the mountains, and, therefore, do not, as I should have liked to find, correspond with the description of the Fountain of the Caledonian Merlin, given in the *Vita Merlini*, of the 12th century, ascribed to Geoffrey of Monmouth. But in crossing the mountains here, that central mountain-district of the east of Scotland, which separates Tweeddale from Annan-dale and Moffat-dale, and where, at no great distance apart, are to be found the sources of the eastward-flowing Tweed, the westward-running Clyde, and the southward-falling Annan, I found many other fountains to which Geoffroy's (?) lines would apply:

> " Fons erat in summo cujusdam vertice montis,
> Undique præcinctus corulis, densisque frutectis,
> Illic Merlinus consederat; inde per omnes
> Spectabat silvas, cursusque, jocosque ferarum."[82]

[81] Villemarqué, *Merlin*, p. 234.

[82] *Vita Merlini*, ll. 138–141 in San-Marte (Schultz) *Die Sagen von Merlin*, p. 277.

After journeying past deep ravines, and shadowy mountain nooks;
through dales, over the steep green sides of which swept the swift
shadows of the clouds, and fell, in silver torrents, many a waterfall;
through a country, in which the long presence of a large Saxon
element in its population was witnessed-to by the vulgarity of the
names — Devil's Beef-tub, Grey Mare's Tail, etc.—by which so
many of its finest scenes were profaned;[83] I passed a night at the
famous cottage of Tibbie Shiels, where I was sorry to find the old
housekeeper of the Ettrick Shepherd on her death-bed; and so, the
next day, on, through Ettrick Forest.　Somewhere in this district
must have been fought Arthur's seventh battle "'in silva Caledonis
id est cat Coit Celeddon,'—that is, the battle was so called, for
Cat means 'battle,' and *Coed Celyddon*, 'the wood of Celyddon.'
. . . . of which the forests of Selkirk and Ettrick formed a part;"[84]
and which is mentioned along with the Teifi or Teviot in a poem
relating to the battle of Arderydd in the *Black Book of Caermarthen.*

> " Seven score generous ones have gone to the shades;
> In the wood of Celyddon they came to their end."[85]

On the Teviot, also, Mr. Pearson[86] places the Din Guortigern, mentioned by Nennius.

Coming to Melrose by Abbotsford we pass through the Rhymer's
Glen and by the Huntly Burn :

> "True Thomas lay on Huntlie bank;
> A ferlie he spied wi' his ee;
> And there he saw a ladye bright,
> Come riding down by the Eildon Tree."[87]

---

[83] " As the Saxon names of places, with the pleasant wholesome smack of the soil
in them—Weathersfield, Thaxted, Shalford—are to the Celtic names of places, with
their penetrating lofty beauty—Velindra, Tyntagel, Caernarvon,—so is the homely
realism of German and Norse nature to the fairy-like loveliness of Celtic nature."—
ARNOLD, *Study of Celtic Literature,* p. 159. Sir Walter Scott certainly makes the
best of the *Grey Mare's Tail* when he says of this cataract of 200 feet that it,
> " White as *the snowy charger's tail,*
> 　　Drives down the pass of Moffatdale."—*Marmion, Introd. to Canto* 2.
[84] *Four Ancient Books,* v. I. p. 54.　　[85] Ibid. v. I. p. 370 ; v. II. pp. 18 and 337.
[86] *Historical Maps—Britannia Cambrica.*
[87] SCOTT, *Minstrelsy of the Scotish Border.　Thomas the Rhymer,* Part 1.

Immediately to the south of Melrose, the Melros of Nennius, rise those
three summits of the Eildons, the *Tremontium* of the Romans, which
Mr. Nash identifies with the Din Drei of Aneurin, and near which he
places the site of the battle celebrated in the *Gododin*.[88] These three
summits also with their various weirdly appurtenants—the Windmill
of Kippielaw, the Lucken Hare, and the Eildon Tree—mark the
domes of those vast subterranean Halls, in which all the Arthurian
Chivalry await, in an enchanted sleep, the bugle-blast of the Adventurer who will call them at length to a new life. And it is to be
noted also that there are on the Eildons the remains of a fortified
camp, and at their foot a Bowden Burn and Bowden Moor, at the
further end of which is another hill with the remains of fortifica-
tions. There is not, however, an Avon here to enable us to oppose
this site to that which Mr. Skene has identified as the *Mons Badonis*
of Arthur's twelfth battle.

Crossing the winding Tweed, we find " six miles to the west of
that heretofore noble and eminent monastery of Meilros," Gwaedol,
or " Wedale, in English Wodale, in Latin Vallis Doloris." Here, at
Stowe, was the church of Saint Mary, where were once "preserved,
in great veneration, the fragments of that image of the Holy Virgin,
Mother of God," which Arthur, on his return from Jerusalem,[89]
" bore upon his shoulders, and through the power of our Lord Jesus
Christ, and the Holy Mary, put the Saxons to flight, and pursued
them the whole day with great slaughter." [90] Not far from this
church at Stowe, dedicated to S. Mary, General Roy places a Roman
fort; and thus the site of Arthur's eighth battle " in Castello

---

[88] *On the History of the Battle of Cattraeth and the Gododin of Aneurin*, in *The
Cambrian Journal*, 1861.

[89] Pilgrims from Britain are mentioned by S. Jerome. There is, therefore, no
historical improbability in the legends of Arthur's pilgrimage to the Holy Sepulchre.

[90] *Harleian MS.* of the *Historia Britonum*. Henry of Huntingdon, who likewise
gives this account, says the image was upon his shield; and, as in Welsh, *ysgwyd* is a
shoulder, and *ysgwydd*, a shield, a Welsh original must have been differently translated by the two authors.

Guinnion " is very plainly indicated.[91]   This Guinnion also appears
in the Garanwynyon mentioned in the poem in the *Book of Taliessin*
on the battle of Gwenystrad or the White Strath, thus also identified
with the valley of the Gala Water.

> " In defending Gwenystrad was seen
> A mound and slanting ground obstructing
> .   .   .   .   .   .
> Hand on the cross they wail on the gravel bank of Garanwynyon."

And the White Stone of Galystem (in which the name Gala seems
contained), referred to in the succeeding lines,

> " I saw a brow covered with rage on Urien,
> When he furiously attacked his foes at the White Stone
> Of Galystem," [92]

is probably the stone mentioned in the *Statistical Account* : " A little
above it (S. Mary's Church of Stow) is a very fine perennial spring,
known by the name of the Lady's Well, and a huge stone, recently
removed in forming the new road, but now broken to pieces, used
to be pointed out as impressed with the print of the Virgin Mary's
foot."   In the Verses of the Graves also this valley seems to be
alluded to.[93]

Crossing from Stowe to Lauder, and journeying down the Leader
Water we come to the Rhymer's Tower, on a beautiful haugh or
meadow by the waterside.   Here in his Castle of Ercildoune, of
which these are the ruins, lived Thomas the Rhymer, whom so many
traditions connect with Arthurian Romance, in representing him as
the unwilling, and too quickly vanishing guide of those adventurous
spirits who have entered the mysterious Halls beneath the Eildons,
and attempted to achieve the re-awakening of Arthur and his
knights, but only to be cast forth, amid the thunders of the fateful
words :—

> " Woe to the Coward that ever he was born,
> Who did not draw the Sword, before he blew the Horn." [94]

---

[91] *Four Ancient Books*, v. I. p. 55. [92] Ibid. v. I. pp. 343-4.
[93] Ibid. v. II. p. 412.
[94] See *Appendix to General Preface to Waverley*.

And hence it is to "True Thomas," still "doomed to revisit Eildon's fated Tree," that Leyden appeals to

> " Say who is he with summons long and high,
> Shall bid the charméd sleep of Ages fly ;
> Roll the long sound through Eildon's caverns vast,
> While each dark warrior kindles at the blast ;
> The Horn, the Falchion grasp with mighty hand,
> And peal proud Arthur's march from Fairyland." [95]

From Ercildoune, or Earlston, we journey to Kelso, which is mentioned in the *Book of Taliessin* as Calchvynyd.[96] This literally means "Chalk mountain," and Chalmers says, "It seems to have derived its ancient name of Calchow from a calcareous eminence which appears conspicuous in the middle of the town, and which is still called the Chalk Heugh." [97] At no great distance to the south of Kelso is Jedburgh, identified by Mr. Pearson with the Judeu and Atbret Judeu of Nennius ;[98] and Mr. Nash and the Ven. Archdeacon Jones, placing Manau Guotodin further south than Mr. Skene would do, extend it beyond Jedburgh, and so as to include Northumberland. [99]

Though properly, perhaps, belonging to the next district, we shall find it more convenient to include in our exploration of *Tweed-dale* that river Glen, one of the indirect tributaries of the Tweed, which the above-quoted writer in the *Gentleman's Magazine* identifies with the Glein or Gleni, at the mouth of which took place the first battle in which Arthur was engaged. "Near the junction of the Glen with the Till rises a lofty hill, called from its shape 'Weavering Bell,' on the summit of which are to be seen to this day the remains of a rude fortress of immense strength, and nearly inaccessible position. The hill rises abruptly to the height of upwards of 2000

---

[95] *Scenes of Infancy*, Part II.
[96] *Four Ancient Books*, v. I. p. 363, and v. II. p. 162.
[97] *Caledonia*, v. II. p. 146.
[98] *Historical Maps—Britannia Cambrica.*
[99] *On the History of the Battle of Cattraeth*, etc., in *The Cambrian Journal*, 1861.

feet, the summit being attained by a winding path on its south-east side, and presenting a level plain of about 12 acres. . . . . . In the midst is an elevated citadel. . . . . . That this was at a later period a royal fortress of the Saxons we know on the authority of Bede. . . . . . And that Weavering was a fortress of the Britons, before it fell into the hands of the Saxons . . . . . is supported by the tradition of ages. . . . . . On the invasion of their country by a superior force, the Ottodeni naturally sought refuge in this fortress. . . . . . In their behalf, Arthur first drew his sword upon the Saxons. . . . . . Its position near the capital of Bernicia, and its celebrity from the ministration of Paulinus and the narrative of Bede, account for this river being mentioned without any allusion (as in the case of the Duglas) to the region in which it flowed." [100]

Along the Border-country we note an almost endless number of places, famous in story, among which we must, at least, name Carham as the scene of the battle which finally added the Saxon Lothians to the Celtic kingdom of Malcolm II. in 1018.[101] And so, on to Berwick, formerly Aberwick. And, though now fallen into comparative decay and insignificance,—crowning, as it does, the northern heights at the mouth of the Tweed, looking eastward on the sea, that dashes up to high caverned cliffs, and commanding westward the vale of the beautiful river, here flowing between steep braes, shadowy with trees, or bright with corn and pasture, —Berwick, but for the dulness within its walls, seems still almost as worthy of being called Joyeuse Garde as, both from its real and romance history of siege, conquest, and reconquest, it is of being remembered as Dolorous Garde.[102]

---

[100] *Gentleman's Magazine,* v. XVII. (1842), p. 59.

[101] See ROBERTSON, *Scotland under Her Early Kings,* v. I. p. 96, n.

[102] See SCOTT, *Romance of Sir Tristrem, Introduction,* p. xxxvii. See also BURTON, *History of Scotland,* v. I. p. 177.

SECTION (II).

The Southern Division of Arthurian Scotland.

From the still preserved ramparts of Berwick I observed, away to
the south, a great pyramid-like mass by the sea; and, on asking
what this was, I was told it was Bamborough Castle.   "Ah,"
said I to myself, "the Chatel Orgueilleux of Romance [103] and the
Dinguaroy and Bebbanburgh of Nennius."   So, entering on the
exploration of *District IV.—Northumberland,* I went by train to
the Belford station, whence it is some five miles to the little model
village under the Castle-rock.   And whatever may on other grounds
be said of the expenditure of the funds vested for certain charit-
able purposes in the Trustees to whom this ancient Castle, with
its valuable estates, now belongs, an Arthurian antiquary can
hardly but be grateful to them for enabling him to enter, what
might easily be imagined one of the very castles of which he has
been reading.   Occupying the whole extent of a solitary eminence,
it stands among sandy downs, close by the sea, and overlooking
a wide plain at the foot of the Cheviots.   Nearly opposite the
Castle are the Faroe Islands.   And journeying five or six miles
over the sands when the tide is out, and a mile by boat, one reaches
Lindisfarne, the Medgaud of Nennius, opposite which, on the mainland, is the Lleu.   Having visited the Abbey of the Holy Island of
St. Cuthbert,—like Iona, whence the saintly Aidan came here as a
missionary, a primitive seat of Christianity,—and where, as I
thought, there ought to have been a tradition of its having been
the retreat of Sir Lancelot after the discovery of his treason, and
his final separation from the Queen; I regained the mainland, and
Beal station, in a slow, jolting cart, chased by the too swiftly
incoming tide, but amusing myself thinking of the still worse

---

[103] SCOTT, *Romance of Sir Tristrem, Introduction,* p. xxxvii.

jolting Sir Lancelot underwent, and the ludicrous disgrace brought upon him by his accepting the offer of the dwarf to guide him to the captive Guenivere, would the knight but leave his disabled horse, and get into "la charette," the filthy cart of the dwarf.[104]

The references to Northumberland in the Romances are very frequent. It was in the forest of Northumberland that dwelt the Hermit Blaise to whom Merlin is represented as so often repairing, in order that being "a nobill clerk and subtle," he might put in writing all the wonderful things that befell in those days. And one chapter, for instance, of the French Romance of Lancelot is headed, "Comment la Dame de Noehault envoya deuers le Roy Artus, luy supplier quil luy envoya secours contre le Roy de Norhombellande qui luy menoit guerre." Northumberland also formed part of the Berneich of Nennius, the Tir Brenech of Llywarch Hen, and the Brenneich of Aneurin, the Anglic kingdom of Bernicia. And in the suburbs of its chief town, Newcastle, we find Arthur's Hill.

We are now on the Tyne, the south-eastern boundary of Arthurian Scotland. But, before turning westward, we must note that, but a little way over the frontier is York, Eboracum, with which the name of the father of Perceval, that famous knight of the Quest of the Holy Grail is connected. For he is always mentioned as Ebrauk or Evrok of the North.[105] But, under his earlier Cymric name of Peredur, Perceval is brought into more direct connection with Arthurian Scotland in his relations with Merlin in the Caledonian Forest—

> " Venerat ad bellum Merlinus cum Pereduro
> ·   ·   ·   ·   ·   ·   ·   ·   ·   ·   ·
> Solatur Peredurus eum,"—[106]

[104] From this adventure a metrical romance, composed by Chestien de Troyes in the twelfth century, takes its title *La Charette.*

[105] VILLEMARQUE, *Romans de la Table Ronde*, pp. 321 and 395.

[106] *Vita Merlini*, l. 31 and l. 68. SAN MARTE (SCHULTZ), *Die Sagen von Merlin*, pp. 274-5.

and as one of the chiefs mentioned by Aneurin in the *Gododin* as having fallen at the battle of Cattraeth:

> "Peredur with steel arms, Gwawrddur, and Aeddan,
> A defence were they in the tumult, though with shattered shields."[107]

Turning now westward, and passing through the picturesquely-situated old town of Hexham, with its Moot Hall and Abbey Church, on a wooded ridge over-hanging the Tyne, we stop either at the Haydon Bridge, or the Bardon Mill station of the Carlisle and Newcastle Railway. For six or eight miles to the north of these stations, and in the neighbourhood of Housesteads, the most complete of the stations on the Roman Wall, are the principal Arthurian Localities of this Northumbrian District. The scenery here is very remarkable. The green, but unwooded grazing hills,—wide and wild-looking from their want of enclosures, and the infrequency of farm-houses,—seem like the vast billows of a north-sweeping tide. Along one of these wave-lines runs the Roman Wall, with the stations of its garrison. In the trough, as it were, of this mighty sea, and to the north of the Wall, were, till a few years ago removed and ploughed over, the ruins of the ancient castle of Sewing Shields, referred to by Sir Walter Scott as the Castle of the Seven Shields,[108] and by Camden as Seavenshale.[109] Beneath it, as under the Eildons, Arthur and all his court are said to lie in an enchanted sleep. And here also tradition avers that the passage to these Subterranean Halls, having once on a time, been found, but the wrong choice having been made in the attempt to achieve the adventure, and call the Chivalry of the Table Rounde to life again, the unfortunate adventurer was cast forth with these ominous words ringing in his ears:

---

[107] *Four Ancient Books*, v. I. p. 386. Compare also Guest (Lady Charlotte *Mabinogion, Notes to Peredur the Son of Evrawc*, v. I. p. 371.

[108] *Harold the Dauntless*, s. VI.

[109] Bruce, *The Roman Wall*, p. 175.

" O woe betide that evil day
   On which this witless wight was born,
   Who drew the Sword, the Garter cut,
   But never blew the Bugle-horn"—[110]

the very opposite mistake, it will be observed, to that of which the equally luckless Eildon adventurer was guilty.

The northern faces of three successive billows here, if I may so call them, present fine precipitous crags,—whinstone and sandstone strata cropping out. These are called respectively Sewing Shields Crags, the King's, and the Queen's Crags. Along the crest of the first of these the Roman Wall is carried. The others take their name from having been the scene of a little domestic quarrel, or tiff, between King Arthur and Queen Quenivere. To settle the matter, the king sitting on a rock called Arthur's Chair, threw at the queen an immense boulder which, falling somewhat short of its aim, is still to be seen on this side of the Queen's Crags. And on the horizon of the immense sheep farm of Sewing Shields, and beyond an outlying shepherd's hut, very appropriately named Coldknuckles, is a great stone called Cumming's Cross, to which there is attached another rude Arthurian tradition. For here, they say, that King Arthur's sons attacked, and murdered a northern chieftain who had been visiting their father at Sewing Shields Castle, and who was going home with too substantial proofs, as they thought, of the king's generosity.

Thence, over a most bracingly wild, wide-horizoned, and open Border-country to Liddesdale.[111] At the head of this famous dale we find Dawston, which may be reckoned among localities of the Arthurian Age, as the scene of that great battle of Dagsestan of 603, in which Aidan, who seems to have been, like Arthur some sixty years before, performing the functions of *Guledig* or "Dux

---

[110] HODGSON, *History of Northumberland*, Part II. v. III. p. 287.

[111] Liddesdale is, of course, known to be within the political frontier of Scotland, though its Arthurian localities are here treated of partly as belonging to the district of Northumberland, and partly to that of Cumberland.

Bellorum" in the North, led a combined force of Scots and Britons against the Angles of Bernicia, under Ethelfrid; only, however, to meet with a crushing defeat.[112]

But our next and more strictly Arthurian locality, a hill, on the eastern side of the valley, called Arthur's Seat—the third locality of that name we have found in the course of our journey—we must place in *District V.—Cumberland.* The chief object, however, of our exploration of Liddesdale, is the locality of the great battle of Arderydd, so often mentioned in the *Four Ancient Books,* in the *Triads,* and in the *Vita Merlini.* "Concealed under these extravagant fables, we can see," says Mr. Skene, "the outlines of one of those great historical struggles which alter the fate of a country. . . . It was, in short, a great struggle between the supporters of the advancing Christianity and the departing Paganism, in which the former were victorious. That it was an historical event, and that this was its character, appears from this, that it occurs in the *Annales Cambriæ,* as a real event about the year 573; 'Bellum Armterid inter filios Elifer et Gwendoleu filium Keidiau in quo bello Gwendoleu cecidit. Merlinus insanus effectus est;' and that 573 is the first year of the reign of Rhydderch over Strathclyde, and of Aidan, over Dalriada,"[113]—these being the leaders of the Christian party.

Where, then, was this battle fought? It was a passage in the *Vita S. Kentigerni,* quoted by M. de la Villemarqué,[114] that induced me to look in Liddesdale for its site. Shortly before, however, the same passage had been similarly suggestive to Mr. Skene;

---

[112] *Four Ancient Books,* v. I. pp. 177-8; also v. II. p. 365, where it is said that Mr. Stephens now considers this battle to have been that celebrated in the poems of the Gododin. Donald Brec, who was defeated in the battle of Strathcawin,—the subject, according to Mr. Skene, of the second part of these poems,—was the son of this Aidan.

[113] *Notice of the Site of the Battle of Arderyth—Proceedings of the Society of Antiquaries of Scotland,* v. VI. P. I. p. 95 (published in 1867, my visit being in 1866).

[114] *Myrdhin, ou L'Enchanteur Merlin,* p. 72.

though his *Notice of the Site of the Battle of Arderyth* was not published till after the identification which was the result of my visit to the place. This passage is as follows. One day that the saint was praying in a wild solitude of the Caledonian Forest, there sprang across his path " quidam demens, nudus et hir sutus, ab omni solatio mundiali destitutus, quasi quoddam torvum furiale." The saint asked this strange being who, or what he was, and received for answer, " Olim Quortigerni vates, Merlinus vocitatus, in hac solitudine dura patiens. . . . . . Eram enim cædis omnium causa interemptorum qui interfecti sunt in bello, cunctis in hac patria constitutis satis noto, quod erat *in campo inter Lidel et Carvanolow situato.*" [115]

Carwhinelow is a burn, on which there is a village of the same name, and which flows from Nicholl Forest into the Esk. And some little way above the junction of the Esk, with the Liddel is what is called in the *Statistical Account*, the Moat of Liddel, though known in the country only as the Roman Camp. It is situated on the top of a high bank overhanging the river, to which, on the north side, the rock goes sheer down ; while on the other side it is defended by prodigious earthen ramparts which rise from the field to a height of nearly thirty feet. There is a well in the enclosure, and on the west side a second great rampart. " It is obviously," says Mr. Skene, " a native strength." On its east side the ground slopes down till it comes to the level of the river at a place called Ridding, not quite half a mile off. Between the fort and the village of Carwhinelow is a field extending to the ridge along the stream of that name. This, then, is certainly the " campus inter Lidel et Carwanolow situato." The name of Erydon which Merlin gives to the battle probably remains in Ridding at

[115] *Vita S. Kentigerni*, MSS. Mus. Britann. Cf. FORDUN *Scotichronicon*, lib. III. cxxxi. p. 135, ed. Edinb. 1759. See also SCOTT, Introduction to *Thomas the Rhymer*, Part II., in *Minstrelsy of the Scotish Border*.

the foot of the fort. "And I have no doubt," says Mr. Skene, "that the name Carwhinelow is a corruption of Caerwenddolew, the Caer or city of Gwenddolew,"[116] who, as we have seen, was the leader of the Pagan party, and slain in this battle.

Looking westward from the fort, the eye rests on the gleaming Solway, and southwards, on the knolls of Arthuret, beyond which the Cumberland hills bound the horizon. To Arthuret, then, let us next proceed. For double *d* in Welsh being equivalent to *th*, we can hardly now refuse to recognise in it the name of Arderydd[117] by which the battle is commonly mentioned. Should any doubt remain, it will be dispelled by a visit to the place, which is but some two miles from Longtown. Standing there, on the knolls by Arthuret Church and looking west, with Liddel and Carvanolow behind, a grander battle-plain could hardly be imagined, could the enemy be manœuvred to attack one in a position of which that eminence should be the centre. In the distance behind and around, low hills, except where they rise to a greater height on the Scotish border; in front, the Esk, flowing across the plain, to fall into the Solway Firth, after having been joined by the Line; and bounding the plain, the sea, into which, should the enemy have been unsuccessful in their attack, the victors, fording the river, might drive them in irreparable rout.

At Camelon on the Firth of Forth, we found the site of the battle that closed the career of the historical Arthur in 537. But it was on this scene of the great battle of Arderydd in 573, that it seemed to me, standing on the knolls of Arthuret, that the final Arthurian battle of the Romances might best be imagined to have been fought,—the enemy, driven down from the Moat of Liddel, we have

---

[116] *Notice of the Site*, etc., above quoted, p. 98.

[117] Arthuret, as a name, therefore, has nothing whatever to do with Arthur, as Hutchinson supposes (*History of Cumberland*, v. II. p. 545), making it a corruption of Arthur's head; and is mentioned among these Arthurian localities, not because of its connection with Arthur, but with the Arthurian Merlin.

just visited, here making a last stand. For it is Merlin who is the romantic character, *par excellence* of the Romances; and it seemed fitter to make the scene of the last great battle of the Romance Arthur the same as that in which Merlin, who is in the Romances so intimately connected with Arthur, historically "bore the golden torques," than to make the scene of that battle which, in its event, was the departing out of this world of all the Arthurian chivalry, the same as that in which the historical Arthur fell, but at which Merlin was not present. And, besides, here we have a great Western Lake, which suits that primitive mythological element which can, I think, be shown cropping-out with singular frequency in the Arthurian Romance-cycle.

With such thoughts, then, I wandered over the old battle plain, past great farms, or rather agricultural manufactories, with their steam-engines and chimney-stalks, down to and by a primitive wooden bridge mounted on stilts, across the Line. Then, getting on the turnpike-road to Glasgow, I crossed the Esk by an iron bridge, and, a mile or so on the south side of the border, I turned down towards the sea, but some five minutes distant now. The scene I beheld as I went down to the tide, "washing among the reeds," struck me as of a weird and magical beauty. Behind, in the middle of the great plain, was still clearly visible the mound of Arthuret; before me, in the far distance to the right, was the Scotish Criffel, and, to the left, the English Skiddaw; between these, in the sheen of the setting sun, and stretching away amid points of land to the west, so that, whether it was land-locked as a lake, or boundless as a sea, one could not tell, was the Solway. "Here," I thought, "well may one feign that here, even at such a sunset hour as this, after the last fatal battle on the plain above, Excaliber was thrown into the sea; that here it was caught by the fairy hand, and borne aloft, symbol of the hope, and ultimate triumph of the genius of the Celtic race; and there, in the infinite Beyond, is Avalon."

Coming up to Gretna Green from the Solway, we proceed to Carlisle, which would appear to be the Caer Lliwelydd of the *Book of Taliessin*,[118] and the Cardueil of Romance, evens till more famous than the hardly yet identified Camelot, as the favourite residence of King Arthur. And with reason. For beautifully does the Castle- and Cathedral-crowned eminence, swept round by the Eden, the Peteril, and the Caldew, rise from the wide plain that stretches from the Border Hills down to, and along the Solway Firth. Of the Eden there is a tradition that King Arthur's father tried to turn it out of its course:

> "Let Uther-pendragon do what he can,
> Eden shall run where Eden ran." [119]

But a visit to the populous modern manufacturing quarter, in the evening, when the hands are loose, (how meaningful is the phrase!) may profitably disturb antiquarian memories, and romantic associations.

From Carlisle, near which would appear to have been the Guasmoric of Nennius,[120] our Arthurian pilgrimage takes us southward again through the Inglewood Forest of Romance. From the Southwaite station, we have a walk of something more than two miles, through a beautifully-wooded lane, its waysides luxuriant with wild flowers, to the village of Upper Hesket. At the "White Ox" I had the good fortune to encounter an intelligent old man, who, taking me to the back of the farmyard, pointed out, down in the hollow, what I was in search of, the famous Tarn Wahethelyne of Ballad and Romance. But Tarn Wadling, as it has been called in later times, has been for the last ten years a wide meadow, grazed by hundreds of sheep. Of the

---

[118] *Four Ancient Books*, v. I. p. 257, and v. II. pp. 200 and 419.

[119] As an illustration of the unlikely places in which one may find the objects of one's search, I may note that I found this tradition mentioned in Mr. Mortimer Collins' novel, *Who is the Heir?* v. I. p. 253.

[120] PEARSON, *Historical Maps—Britannia Cambrica.*

draining of it the old man, the innkeeper as it turned out, who had come from Yorkshire, but had been here for the last fifty years, had a great deal to say. Among the rest, what fun it was to see the swine that belonged to a cottager at the far end of the tarn, get tired of the dead carp, that were cast on the land, and wade in to fish for the " quick uns." But of the story of the Grim Baron whom King Arthur chanced to meet here, whose

> —— " Strokes were nothing sweet," [121]

and who refused all other ransom than that the King should, within a year and a day, bring him word " what thing it is that women most desire ; " and of the Foul Ladye who, at length, gave, for the courteous Sir Gawayne's sake, the true answer, and who, on her marriage, was so transformed that

> " The Queen sayd, and her ladyes alle,
> She is the fayrest nowe in this halle ;"—

of how

> " This ferly byfelle fulle sothely to fayne
> In Iggillwode Foreste at the Tarn-wathelayne ;" [122]

of all this, neither my old friend nor his dame had ever heard, till, sitting by their kitchen fire to dry my clothes, wet with a heavy shower, I told them the tale. And all he knew about King Arthur was that

> " When as King Arthur ruled this land,
>   He ruled it like a swine ;
> He bought three pecks of barleymeal
>   To make a pudding fine.
> " His pudding it was nodden well,
>   And stuffed right full of plums ;
> And lumps of suet he put in
>   As big as my two thumbs ;"—

a tradition of the " Flos Regum," hitherto, I believe, unnoticed.

Crossing the south end of the Tarn, or rather meadow, and passing through a fir wood, I ascended Blaze Fell, and, from the quarry on

[121] MADDEN, *Romances of Sir Gawayne* (Bannatyne Club).
[122] Ibid.

its summit, had a fine view over the undulating, mountain bounded, and still finely wooded ancient forest of Inglewood. Below me was the Tarn; to the west of it, the ridge of Upper Hesket; to the east, an eminence with the site, though no more the ruins, of the Castle Hewin of Romance, the stronghold of the Grim Baron. And behind this eminence the Eden flows past still another locality that recalls his fame, and, with it, the legend of the Marriage of Sir Gawayne, —Baron-wood. This legend belongs, as I think, to the class of Sun-myths; and it may be instructive to compare with it that of the Laidley Worm of Spindleston Heugh, near Bamborough Castle, celebrated in the ballad of 1270 by Duncan Frazier the Bard of Cheviot. As the Foul Lady is transformed into "the fairest in hall," so also is the Laidley Worm, or Loathsome Dragon. For her brother, coming over the Eastern Sea, in a ship with Rowan-tree masts,

> ". . . . sheathed his sword, and bent his bow,
> And gave her kisses three;
> She crept into a hole a Worm,
> And stepped out a Ladye." [123]

Returning to the Southwaite Station, we proceed next to Penrith, passing on our way the Plumpton Park and Hatton Hall which Sir Frederic Madden identifies with places of similar names in the Romances of Sir Gawayne.[124] Thence, crossing the narrow but picturesque old bridge of the Eamont, which, flowing from Ulleswater, here separates the counties of Westmoreland and Cumberland, we find, closely adjoining the fine Celtic monument of Mayborough, another such set of circular embankments round a flat-surfaced central mound as we found, but on a larger scale, under the battlements of Stirling Castle. But what is there now called the King's Knot, is here named Arthur's Round Table. And, connected with a cave in the demesne of Brougham Castle in this neigh-

[123] See WHITE, *Northumberland and the Border*, p. 249 et seq. Compare also FERGUSSON, *Tree and Serpent Worship*, p. 32, n.

[124] MADDEN, *Romances of Syr Gawayne*, p. 309.

bourhood, we still find a tradition of a giant killed by the most famous knight of the Table Rounde, Sir Lancelot du Lac. Continuing our journey, we come on the Winster, which is another stream separating the counties of Cumberland and Westmoreland, and would appear to be the Gwensteri of the *Book of Taliessin*; [125] as the Derwent should seem to be the Derwennydd of the *Gododin Poems*. [126]

Here we have come to the south-western limit of what I venture to designate Arthurian Scotland. And now, turning northwards, again, I determined, if possible, to verify Sir F. Madden's conjecture that the Grene Chapel spoken of in the Scotish Romance of *Syr Gawayne and the Grene Knight* (by "Huchowne of the Awle Ryale" [127]?) is the same with the "Chapel of the Grene," which, in the older maps of Cumberland, is marked as existing on the point of land on the western coast, running into the estuary of the Wampool, not far from Skinburness. So from Silloth, which seems to be getting a favourite sea-bathing and health-recruiting place, I wandered up the Solway beach to the extreme point of Skinburness. And this much, at least, by way of verification of Sir F. Madden's conjecture, I may say, that there is near this a beautifully embayed shore, covered with the brightest green down to the very water's edge, from which, if, indeed, the site of the Chapel of the Grene, it might well have taken its name; and, further, that Volsty or Vulstey Castle, so long associated with the necromantic fame of the wizard Michael Scott, and which once stood in the fair wide plain which rises gradually to the foot of Skiddaw, might, from its site with reference to this bright green shore, the seaward border of the plain, well be that in which Sir Gawayne took up his abode, and which is stated to have been but two miles distant from the Grene Chapel, the object of his quest.

[125] *Four Ancient Books*, v. I. p. 338, and v. II. p. 402.
[126] Ibid. v. I. p. 406, v. II. p. 449.
[127] MADDEN, *Romances of Syr Gawayne.*

Away, from here, over the sea, is the Castle of the King of Man—

> "He lett him see a castle faire,
> Such a one he neuer saw yare,
> Noe wher in noe country.
> The Turke said to Sir Gawaine,
> 'Yonder dwells the King of Man,
> A heathen soldan is hee.' "[128]

And the Isle of Man, is the Mynaw of Taliessin;[129] the Manau and Eubonia of Nennius.[130]   May it possibly be also the Ermonie of the *Romance of Sir Tristrem?*   Merlin, at any rate, is traditionally connected with the Isle of Man, as well as Gawayne.   For, by Merlin the giants, who had overpowered the primitive population of Fairies, are in their turn said to have been overpowered, and spell-bound in subterranean chambers.[131]

A shower falling with the turn of the tide, I took shelter in a little cottage, where I found a pretty young woman with her first-born in her arms.   Crowing, instead of crying, at sight of the stranger, I remarked what a fine big boy he was ; and his proud mother, turning her face modestly a little away, replied: "And yet they say that foresons are ordinarily sma'."   Looking from the cottage door, she pointed out to me where, on the opposite shore of the gleaming water, Annan might just be distinguished, and where, up the estuary of the Nith, lay Dumfries.   And I was delighted with the beautiful lake-like Firth; the charm of which, I imagined, must be mainly owing to the variety of its coast-outlines, and the undefined, mysterious recesses of its bays and estuaries; though

---

[128] MADDEN, *Romances of Syr Gawayne.*   See also *Bishop Percy's Folio MS.,* v. I. p. 95.

[129] PEARSON, *Historical Maps—Britannia Cambrica.*

[130] " Tres magnas insulas habet, quarum una vergit contra Armoricas, et vocatur Inisgueith ; secunda sita est in umbilico maris inter Hiberniam et Britanniam et vocatur nomen ejus Eubonia, id est Manau." This name was also, as we have above seen, applied to a district in North Britain ; "regio qui vocatur Manau Guotodin." It should seem that "the island was associated with the name of the Scots, and the region with that of the Picts." *Four Ancient Books,* v. I. p. 83.

[131] See WALDRON, *History and Description of the Isle of Man.*

there were also, indeed, the fine distant forms of the Scotish and
English mountains, and the lights and shades of a bright, though
beclouded summer's day.

Returning to Carlisle, thence crossing the Border, and turning along
the northern shore of the Solway, the Galwudiæ Mare of Gildas,[132] we
enter *District VI.—Galloway;* including under that name the western
part of Dumfriesshire, Kirkcudbrightshire, and Wigtonshire. This
district is mentioned in the poems of the Arthurian age as *Gallwyddel*,
of which *Galgaidel* is the Gaelic, and *Galweithia* the Latin form, or equivalent;[133] and it may be described as lying between the Nith and Loch
Ryan.[134] In the Mediæval romances, it is referred to as the patrimony of Sir Gawayne,[135] son of Loth, or Lothus, King of
Lothian. And thus Galloway may be viewed also as the birthland
of the many other knights of whom the only description is but such
as this: "al they were of Scotland, outher of Syr Gawaynes'
kynne, outher well-willers to his brethren."[136]

The localities, however, which we have to note in this, as also
in the next district, belong rather to the Arthurian age than to King
Arthur. But the first two I have to mention may be considered as
exceptions to this rule, as they refer to S. Kentigern, whom so many
traditions connect with Merlin. At Hoddam or Hodelem on the
Annan, it is stated by Joceline[137] that this saint, on his recall from
Wales, after the great Christian victory of Arderydd, placed, for
a time, his episcopal seat. And some way higher up on the opposite side of the river is a church dedicated to him as S. Mungo.
The whole of Nithsdale, and the country about Lochmaben appears
in the *Book of Taliessin*, under the name of Mabon;[138] and Lochar
Moss (near which we may visit the famous Caer-laverock Castle,

[132] *De Excid. Brit.* c. xi. [133] *Four Ancient Books*, v. II. p. 452, etc.
[134] Ibid. p. 401. [135] MADDEN, *Romances of Syr Gawayne.*
[136] MALORY, *The Byrth, Lyf, and Actes of Kyng Arthur.*
[137] *Vita S. Kentigerni* in PINKERTON'S *Vitæ Antiqissimorum Sanctorum.*
[138] *Four Ancient Books*, v. I. pp. 363, 562 and v. II. pp. 420-6.

where Murdoch, second Duke of Albany, was for a time a prisoner in 1425), should seem to be the Man-Llachar of these poems.[139] Near Dumfries, with its tragical memories of the later years, and prema~~ture death, of Burns, we find on the north bank of the Cludon,—the~~ Cludvein or Cledyfein of the poems,—where it falls into the Nith, the scene of the battle also commemorated in the *Book of Taliessin*, where

> "lay the Peithwyr prostrate
> At the end of the wood of Celyddon." [140]

For the author of the *Statistical Account* says, "The lower part of this parish was unquestionably at an early period a *quercetum*, or oak-forest, extending most probably to Snaid, a distance of eight miles." It was termed the Holywood, and a monastery was afterwards founded here called "Abbatia Sacri Nemoris." Not more than a quarter of a mile south-west of the church eleven large stones are placed in an oval form. They are situated near the lower end of the Sacred Grove; and should seem to be a record of this battle of Pencoed. The Peithwyr were no doubt the Picts of Galloway.[141] The Carron which flows into the Nith, in the upper part of its course, is probably the stream mentioned in the same *Ancient Book* as the "boundary of Garant."[142] And the Caer Rywc, mentioned in another of these poems, "probably refers to Sanquhar or Senchaer, the old city which is on the Crawick, a name formed from Caer Rawick as Cramond is from Caer Amond.[143]

Journeying westward past the mediæval ruins of Sweetheart Abbey, of romantic fame, and Kirkcudbright, with its pre-mediæval memories of S. Cuthbert, we come to Wigton; and near this we find what would appear to be the tomb of that Gwallawg ap Lleenawg, relating to whom there is a whole class of poems in the *Four Ancient Books*.[144] For "in the highway between Wigton and Port-

[139] *Four Ancient Books.*
[141] Ibid. v. II. p. 402.
[143] Ibid. v. II. p. 401.

[140] Ibid. v. I. p. 338.
[142] Ibid. v. I. p. 429, and v. II. p. 407.
[144] Ibid. v. I. p. 336 *et seq.*

patrick about three miles westward of Wigton is a plaine called the
Moor of the Standing Stones of Torhouse, in which there is a monument of three large whinstones, called King Galdus's Tomb, surrounded, at about twelve feet distance, with nineteen considerable
great stones, but none of them so great as the three just mentioned,
erected in a circumference." [145]   And of Galdus, or Gallawg, Boece
says "Elatum est corpus . . . . . in vicino campi ut vivens manda-
verat, est conditum ubi ornatissimum ei monumentum patrio more,
immensis ex lapidibus est erectum ; " [146] and he identifies him with
Galgacus who fought against Agricola.[147]   Leaving Whithorn, or
Candida Casa, with its memories of the apostolic S. Ninian, to the
south, we journey on, passing Kirkcowan, with the query whether
there is here to be found a topographical record of Gawayne, and
come at length to the neighbourhood of Loch Ryan.   Here there
seems to be a record of the

" Battle in the Marsh of Terra, at the dawn," [148]

in "four large unpolished stones placed erect and forming a circle.
At a distance of some yards stands a single stone.   They are called
by the country people the 'Standing Stones of Glenterra.' "   Near
this, "about three feet deep in a peat moss, there is a regular pile
of stepping-stones, extending about a quarter of a mile.   These
must have been placed in this position to form a passage through a

---

[145] SYMSON, *Description af Galloway* (1684).

[146] Quoted in *Four Ancient Books*, v. I. p. 171.

[147] The antiquarian controversy about the Mons Grampius, and the site of the battle
between Galgacus and Agricola is well known. See BURTON, *History of Scotland*,
v. I. p. 12 et seq.   But, if I am not deceived by the partiality of a grandson, a very
probable case seems to be made out for that site on the Grampians in the neighbourhood of Stonehaven in Kincardineshire, where we find, on the plain, within a mile
of the sea, a Roman Camp, and directly opposite, on the face of the hills, at the
distance of not more than two miles, a native, or Caledonian entrenchment (Re-
dykes). STUART (of Inchbreck), *Essays on Scotish Antiquities*, pp. 79-80 *et seq.*
See also ROY, *Military Antiquities, Introduction*, p. iv.

[148] *Four Ancient Books*, v. I. p. 338.

swamp previous to the growth of the peat moss." [149]   It remains but
to add that Caer Rheon, now Cairnryan, Llwch Rheon, now Loch
Ryan, and Rhyd Rheon, or Ford of Ryan, are all mentioned in these
poems of the Arthurian Age; [150] and that the Mull of Galloway is
the Novant of Aneurin. [151]

SECTION (III).

The Western Division of Arthurian Scotland.

We now enter on *District VII.—Ayr.* And here we have first to
note that the three immemorial divisions of this county—Carrick,
Kyle, and Cunningham, all appear in the poems of the Arthurian
Age under the more primitive Cymric forms of Carrawg, Coel, and
Canowan.   In the *Book of Taliessin*, [152] we find

> " Of the many-citied Cymri, Carawg,
> The father of Caradawg."

This Caradawg is obviously the Caractacus of Boece, who appears
to have used local traditions whenever he could find them, and who
says that in Carrick " erat civitas tum maxima a qua Caractani regio
videtur nomen sortita. In ea Caractacus natus, nutritus, educatus." [153]
"And a similar monument to that we have found in Galloway to
the memory of Galdus, is described in a MS. quoted by Dr.
Jamieson, in his edition of Bellenden's *Boece* as existing in Carrick.
'There is 3 werey grate heapes of stonnes, callit wulgarley the
Kernes of Blackinney, being the name of the village and ground.
At the suthirmost of thir 3 cairnes are ther 13 great tall stonnes,
standing upright in a perfyte circkle, about some 3 elle ane distaunt
from ane other, with a gret heighe stonne in the midle, which is

---

[149] *Statistical Account of Insch*, in the county of Wigton, quoted in *Four Ancient Books*, v. II. p. 402.

[150] Ibid. v. I. pp. 241, 276, v. II. pp. 337, 401.

[151] PEARSON, *Historical Maps—Britannia Cambrica.*

[152] *Four Ancient Books*, v. I. p. 429.

[153] Quoted, Ibid. v. I. p. 171.

werily esteemed be the most learned inhabitants to be the buriall place of King Caractacus.' "[154]   In reference to this division of Ayr I have only to add that the Gafran of the poems would appear to be Girvan,[155] Caer Caradawg the Caractonium of Boece,[156] and Dunduff the Dindywydd of Aneurin.[157]

In the same poem, and a few lines after those last quoted, we find

> " Who will pay the precious reward ?
> . . . .
> Or Coel, or Canowan ? "[158]

Carrick, Kyle, and Cunningham thus mentioned together.   And in those Verses of the Graves in the *Black Book of Caermarthen*, from which Mr. Arnold takes one of his illustrations of what he calls the *Pindarism* of the Celtic, as contrasted with the *Gemeinheit* of the Teutonic style,[159] we read

> " Whose is the Grave on the slope of the hill ?
> Many who know it do not ask ;
> The Grave of Coel, the son of Cynvelyn."[160]

Boece tells us " Kyl dein proxima est vel Coil potius nominata, a Coilo Britannorum rege ibi in pugna cæso ; "[161] and a circular mound at Coilsfield, in the parish of Tarbolton, on the highest point of which are two large stones, and in which sepulchral remains have been found, is pointed out by local tradition as his tomb.[162]   The

---

[154] Quoted in *Four Ancient Books*, v. I. p. 172.   [155] Ibid. v. II. p. 403.
[156] Ibid. v. II. 415.   [157] PEARSON, *Historical Maps—Britannia Cambrica.*
[158] *Four Ancient Books*, v. I. p. 430.
[159] Ibid. v. I. p. 316, Cynvelyn would become Cymbeline in English.
[160] Ibid. v. I. p. 170.
[161] *Study of Celtic Literature*, p. 145.   The verse he quotes is as follows :
> " The Grave of March is this, and this the Grave of Gwythyr ;
> Here is the grave of Gwgawn Gleddyvrud ;
> But unknown is the Grave of Arthur."
Compare SKENE, *Four Ancient Books*, v. I. p. 315.
[162] Whatever truth there may be in Mr. Fergusson's theory that the so-called Druidical Circles of Britain had nothing whatever to do with the Druids, but are sepulchral monuments of the Arthurian Age ; it seems worth noting that in these Tombs of Gwallawg (Galdus) of Caradawg (Caractacus) and of Coel, we have monuments similar to those elsewhere called Druidical circles, but with traditions attached to them which seem to give support to such a theory as Mr. Fergusson's.

name of "Auld King Coil" is also perpetuated in the Crags of Kyle, the burn of Coyl, and the parish of Coylton.

Coilsfield has fresher, and more romantic memories as the residence, in the humble capacity of a dairy-maid, of Burns' "Highland Mary." For Kyle is the Land of Burns ;[163] as Carrick, we have just left, was the patrimony of Bruce, through the marriage of his father Robert Bruce, son of the Lord of Annandale, with the widowed Countess of Carrick.[164] And local traditions of both the national heroes,—Wallace as well as Bruce having been natives of this south-west part of Scotland,—may not a little have deepened the enthusiastic patriotism of the national poet. But we must proceed with our exploration of that Arthurian stratum of Romance which far underlies all those of mediæval and modern times.

The next locality we have to note is the promontory of Troon, which would appear[165] to be the site of the

"battle in the region of Bretrwyn,"

mentioned in the *Book of Taliessin*.[166] On Dondonald, "in cacumine montis qui appellatur Dundevenel," S. Monenna founded one of her churches after Arthur's victories over the pagan oppressors of his country. And Mr. Skene places his first battle "in ostium fluminis quod vocatur Glein," at the mouth of the river Glen, which rises in the mountains that separate Ayrshire from Lanarkshire, and

---

[163] It must, however, be noted that it was only the father of Burns who migrated to Ayrshire. His ancestors are traceable for three centuries as tenants of farms on the estate of Inchbreck, on the southern slope of the Grampians in Kincardineshire, a property that still belongs to the representative of the Stuarts of Castleton, etc., a branch of the family of the Earl of Castle-Stuart. See *infra*, note 208, p. 89.

[164] Bruce was thus "the representative of a Gaelic line of princes which had ruled over Galloway from time immemorial; whilst his paternal grandfather's mother, through whom he inherited his claim on the throne, was a daughter of the (Gaelic) royal house of Atholl." ROBERTSON, *Scotland under Her Early Kings*, v. II., p. 142 n. The representation of the family of the Bruce passed into that of the Stuarts (*Infra*, p. 89 n. 208); the Bruces, Earls of Elgin, being descended but from a knight of whom all that is known is that he was a cotemporary of the heroic king.

[165] *Four Ancient Books*, v. II. p. 402.

[166] Ibid. v. I. p. 337.

falls into the Irvine in the parish of Loudon. And it appears
to Mr. Skene more probable that "Arthur advanced into Scotland on the West," just as in after days, Bruce, "through the
friendly country peopled by the Cymry, than through Bernicia,"
where, as we have seen,[167] there is another river of this name, but
" which was already occupied by large bodies of Angles."[168]

In Cunningham, the third division of Ayr, and which we have
already noted as mentioned in the poems under the name of
Canowan, was the

> " battle in the wood of Beit at the close of the day,"

referred to by Taliessin.[169] And the place meant would appear to be
the Moor of Beith in this district, where there was formerly a
wood.[170] There should seem, however, to be no other locality of
the Arthurian Age now discoverable here ; so we may turn southwards again, and cross the mountains to the upper waters of the
Clyde.

We now enter *District VIII.—Strathclyde,* "the region of the
Clyd" of the *Red Book of Hergest*.[171] Upper Strathclyde would
appear to be the Arfynydd of the Poems.[172] And here we may
first note that, though, as we found, the Wells of the Tweed
would not, the Sources of the Clyde, on the western slope of the
same mountain-range would, very well accord with the twelfth
century description of the Fountain of the Caledonian Merlin.[173]
But if Merlin's Fountain is not clearly identifiable, we find, in
the parish of Crawford, a well called Arthur's Fountain. That
this name is of very ancient date we have evidence in a grant
of "David de Lindesay, in 1339, to the monks of Newbotle of
the lands of Brotheralwyn in that district which were bounded

---

[167] *Suprà,* p. 72.
[168] *Four Ancient Books,* v. I. p. 52. But see *infrà,* p. 109.
[169] Ibid. v. I. p. 337.   [170] Ibid. v. II. p. 402.
[171] Ibid. v. I. p. 463. See also p. 431, and v. II. p. 399.
[172] Ibid. v. II. p. 413.   [173] *Suprà,* p. 58.

on the west part, "a Fonte Arthuri usque ad summitate montis."[174] And other memories of Merlin are here recalled, for proceeding down the Clyde, we are in the ancient territory of his friend Rydderch Hael. For it is with this king of Strathclyde, not with Arthur, the Guledig, that the historical Merlin is associated. And in one of Merlin's poems relating to the Battle of Arderydd, preserved in the *Black Book of Caermarthen*, he seems to refer to Lanark, in its Cymric form *Llanerch*, a glade,[175] where in one of the apostrophes with which the stanzas of the poem commence, he exclaims—

> " Sweet apple tree that grows in Lanark !
>
> . . . . . .
>
> Sweet apple tree that grows by the river side !"[176]

Overhanging the brawling Avon, and on the skirt of the noble chase which, with its wild cattle and ancient oaks, is all that now remains of that Caledonian Forest, once haunted by Merlin, and which stretched from sea to sea, stands Cadzow Castle. It preserves the name of that district of Godeu, or "regina de Caidzow," as it is called in the life of S. Kentigern, which corresponded with what is now the middle ward of Lanarkshire,[177] and which is so often mentioned in the poems, and particularly in that called the Battle of Godeu :

> " Minstrels were singing,
> Warrior bands were wondering,
> At the exaltation of the Brython,
> That Gwydyon effected."[178]

"This," says Mr. Skene, "was the alliance between the Brython, represented by Lleu (or Lothus) and the Gwyddel by Gwydyon which resulted in the insurrection of Medraut (or Mordred), son of Llew against Arthur, with his combined army of Picts, Britons, and Saxons, and which arose from a section of the Britons in the North

---

[174] *Chart. Newbotle*, N. 148, quoted by CHALMERS, *Caledonia*, v. I. p. 245. See also IRVING and MURRAY, *Upper Ward of Lanarkshire.*

[175] *Four Ancient Books*, v. II. p. 336.

[176] Ibid. v. I. p. 371-2.

[177] Ibid. II. p. 414.   [178] Ibid. v. I. p. 278.

being drawn over to apostasy by the pagan Saxons and semi-pagan Picts." [179]

Calderwood would appear to be the Calaterium Nemus of Geoffrey.[180] Cambuslang is the "regio Lintheamus," or Linthcamus, where S. Cadoc, to whom the parish is dedicated, built a monastery. And the adjoining parish of Carmunnock, formerly Carmannock, preserves the name of the mountain Bannawc—B, in combination, passing into M in Welsh,—mentioned in the life of S. Cadoc, and now called the Cathkin Hills. "Between Strathclyde and Ayrshire lay the district of Strathgryfe, now the county of Renfrew, and this part of Cumbria seems to have been the seat of the family of Caw, commonly called Caw Cawlwydd, or Caw Prydyn, one of whose sons was Gildas.[181] For in one of the lives of Gildas he is said to be the son of Caunus who reigned in Arecluta. . . . . And this name signifies a district lying along the Clyde,"[182] as Strathgryfe or Renfrewshire does.[183] But in Neilston parish, in this county, we find more directly Arthurian localities in the places called Arthur Lee, Low Arthur Lee, and West Arthur Lee.

We conclude our exploration of Strathclyde with Glasgow. It appears in the *Book of Taliessin* as Caer Clud, the City on the Clyde.

" . . . . . they shall pledge the rich plains
From Caer Clud to Caer Caradawg,
The support of the land of Penprys and Gwallawg,
The king of the kings of tranquil aspect." [184]

---

[179] *Four Ancient Books*, v. I. p. 204.

[180] PEARSON, *Historical Maps—Britannia Cambrica.*

[181] Another, the Cueil, or Hueil, king of Scotland, " quem occidit rex Arthurus ?"

[182] *Four Ancient Books*, v. I. p. 173.

[183] It was in this county that the Normanno-Celtic family of the FitzAlans, who, from their hereditary office, took the name of Stewart, had their first grants of lands in Scotland. See SKENE, *History of the Highlanders*, v. II. p. 308 et seq.; and STUART (Hon. and Rev. Godfrey), *Genealogical and Historical Sketch of the Stuarts of the House of Castle-Stuart.* Paisley, the chief town of the county, was founded by Walter Stuart in 1160; and in its Abbey is the tomb of Marjory, daughter of Robert the Bruce, and mother of Robert the Second, the first of the Stuart dynasty.

[184] *Four Ancient Books*, p. 340.

And in a poem in the same Book, connected by its title with the legends of the sons of Llyr, the Lear of Shakspeare, and finely beginning with

> " I will adore the love-diffusing Lord of every kindred,
> The sovereign of hosts manifestly round the Universe,"

Glasgow appears under the name of Penryn Wleth :

> " From Penryn Wleth to Loch Reon
> The Cymry are of one mind, bold heroes." [185]

For " Joceline describes Kentigern as proceeding from the Clyde, and sitting ' super lapidem in supercilio montis vocabulo Gwleth' (c. xiv.) *Gwleth*, forming in combination *Wleth*, signifies dew, and this hill was afterwards known as the Dew or Dowhill in Glasgow." [186] But a better known memorial of the Arthurian founder of the city, three of whose miracles are commemorated on its arms, [187] is S. Mungo's Well, in the crypt of the Cathedral.

We leave Glasgow for the exploration of *District IX.—Lennox.* That part of it to the east of Loch Lomond is identified by Mr. Skene with Murief or Reged. "The district intended by this name appears from a passage in the *Bruts*, where Arthur is said to have driven the Picts from Alclyde into "Mureif, a country which is otherwise termed Reged, and that they took refuge there in Loch Lomond. Loch Lomond was, therefore, in it, and it must have been the district on the North side of the Roman Wall or *Mur*, from which it was called *Mureif.* [188] It is frequently mentioned in the poems ; in one, for instance, in the *Book of Taliessin*, beginning

> " Extol the career of the kings of Reged." [189]

And among special localities in, or adjoining this district may be mentioned Mugdock, in Strathblane, which would appear to be the place meant by the latter of the two names in the line

> " Between Dineiddyn and Dineiddwg," [190]

[185] *Four Ancient Books*, v. I. p. 276.　　　[186] Ibid. v. II. p. 404.
[187] Burton, *History of Scotland*, v. I. p. 249.　　[188] *Four Ancient Books*, v. I. p. 59.
[189] Ibid. p. 350.　　　　　　　　　　　[190] Ibid. p. 270.

the former being clearly Edinburgh.   It was certainly the scene of the great battle of 750 between the Britons of Strathclyde and the Picts at a place called by the Welsh chronicles Magedauc or Maesedauc.[191]   And near this is Ardinny, the scene of the "battle of Ardunnion,"[192] referred to by Taliessin.

On the western brow of the Fintry Hills, we find that "Dun or Down of singular appearance,—its point a perpendicular rock fifty feet high," identified, as above,[193] with the "Height of Adoyn, from which the Bard of the second part of the *Gododin* saw the battle which he describes.   And the Hills of Kilsyth, of which the old form was Kilvesyth, seem to be referred to in the 52nd stanza of the poem—

> " Gododin, in respect of thee will I demand
>   The dales beyond the ridges of *Drum Essyd.*"[194]

Beyond this, along the north-eastern shores of Loch Lomond, Mr. Skene places Argoed Llwyfain.[195]   Here Urien and Owen his son are described in a poem in the *Book of Taliessin* as fighting against Flamddwyn, or the Flamebearer—

> " And because of the affair of Argoed Llwyfain,
>   There was many a corpse.
>   The ravens were red from the warring of men,
>   And the common people hurried with the tidings."[196]

Dumbarton appears to be mentioned under the name of Nemhhur, or Nevtur, in a dialogue between Merlin and Taliessin in the *Black Book of Caermarthen*.[197]   For this name occurs in the *Life of S. Patrick* by Fiech, written in the eight century, after which it is unknown, and is identified by his scholiast with Dumbarton.[198]   And Arthur's ninth battle, "in urbe Leogis qui Britannice Kairlium dicitur," is, by Mr. Skene, added to the innumerable conflicts which have been witnessed by this magnificent fortified rock, where the sword of Wallace is now preserved.   For, as he says, " it seems unlikely that a battle could have been fought at this time with the Saxons at

[191] *Four Ancient Books*, p. 404.   [192] Ibid. p. 337.   [193] *Suprà*, p. 50.
[194] *Four Ancient Books*, v. I. p. 893.   [195] Ibid. v. II. p. 413.
[196] Ibid. v. I. p. 366.   [197] Ibid. v. I. p. 368.   [198] Ibid. II. 321.

either Caerleon on the Esk, or Caerlon on the Dee, which is Chester ;
and these towns Nennius terms, in his list, not Kaerlium or Kaer-
lion, but Kaer Legion.   It is more probably some town in the
north, and the *Memorabilia* of Nennius will afford some indication
of the town intended.   The first of his *Memorabilia* is 'Stagnum
Lumonoy,' or Loch Lomond ; and he adds : 'non vadit ex eo ad
mare nisi unum flumen quod vocatur *Leum*'—that is, the Leven.
The Irish Nennius gives the name correctly, *Leamhuin*, and the Balli-
mote text gives the name of the town, *Cathraig in Leomhan* (for
Leamhan), the town on the Leven.   This was Dumbarton, and the
identification is confirmed by the *Bruts*, which place one of Arthur's
battles at Alclyd ; while his name has been preserved in a parlia-
mentary record of David II. in 1367, which denominates Dumbarton 'Castrum Arthuri.' "[199]   And it may be added that, according
to tradition, it was the birthplace of Mordred, Arthur's nephew or
bastard son.[200]   Under the name of Alclyde, the city on the Clyde—
a name as applicable to it as Kaer Leum, or Cathraig in Leomhan,
for it is at the junction of the Leven with the Clyde,—Dumbarton
is frequently mentioned in the *Four Ancient Books :*

> "A battle in the ford of Alclud, a battle at the Inver." [201]

> "A battle in the ford of Alclud, a battle in the Gwen." [202]

> "There will come from Alclud, men, bold, faithful,
> To drive from Prydein bright armies." [203]

And on the Rock of Clyde, Petra Cloithe, another appropriate name
for Dumbarton, "rex Rodarcus filius Totail regnavit," when, as
recorded by Adomnan,[204] he sent a message to S. Columba, to ask
him, as supposed to possess prophetic power, whether he should be
slain by his enemies.

Lennox, Leven, and Lomond are all one word ; and district, river,

---

[199] *Four Ancient Books,* v. I. pp. 55-6.
[200] CAMPBELL, *West Highland Tales.*
[201] *Four Ancient Books* I. 350.   [202] Ibid. I. 363.
[203] Ibid. I. 441.   [204] *Life of S. Columba.*

and lake are all mentioned in the poems and old historical sources. The original word is, in its Cymric form, *Llwyfain;* in its Gaelic form, *Leamhain,* an elm-tree.   From the latter comes *Leamhanach,* corrupted into Levenachs or Lennox, of which the Cymric equivalent is *Llwyfenydd.*   But the old form of *Leamhan* of which Leven is a corruption, was *Leoman,* with the *m* not as yet aspirated; and from this comes Lomond.   Thus we have the old form adhering to the loch and the mountain, while the river adopts the more modern.[205]   In one of the poems in the *Four Ancient Books* the Lennox is mentioned as having been given to Taliessin in reward for his songs :

> " And a fair homestead,
> And beautiful clothing,
> To me has been extended,
> The lofty Llwyvenydd,
> And requests open." [206]

Sailing up the Lago Maggiore of Scotland there comes, like a dark shadow, across our delight in the loveliness of its fairy islands, the memory of the tragic story connected with the ruins on the largest of them.   For here it was that Isabel, Duchess of Albany lived after the death on the scaffold of her father, her husband, and her two sons,[207] in 1424.   Yet most singular it is, that it is in her, and her husband's descendants, that is the representation of what is now the eldest legitimate male line of the Royal House of Stuart.[208] But proceeding on our voyage, and landing on the western shore of the Lake, about half way up, we find ourselves in Glen Douglas. Here Mr. Skene places Arthur's second third, fourth, and fifth battles

[205] Compare *Four Ancient Books,* v. I. p. 159, and v. II. p. 413.

[206] Ibid. v. I. 347.

[207] To Walter, the younger of the two, the beautiful and pathetic ballad of "Young Waters" is believed, on good ground, to refer.

[208] On the death of Prince Charles Edward without legitimate issue, the eldest son of Robert II. (James I.) was left without descendants in the male line.   The representation, therefore, of the Royal Family of Stuart, as also of that of Bruce, fell to the Earl of Castle-Stuart, the representative in direct male descent of the Duke of Albany, the second son of Robert II., the first of the Dynasty.   See STUART, (Hon.

"super aliud flumen quod dicitur Dubglas et est in regione Linnuis." "Here," says he, "Arthur must have penetrated the 'regiones juxta murum,' occupied by the Saxons. Dubglas is the name now called Douglas. There are many rivers and rivulets of this name in Scotland; but none could be said to be "in regione Linnuis," except two rivers—the Upper and Lower Douglas which fall into Loch Lomond, the one through Glen Douglas, the other at Inveruglas, and which are both in the district of the Lennox, the Linnuis of Nennius. Here, no doubt, the great struggle took place; and the hill called Ben Arthur at the head of Loch Long, which towers over this district between the two rivers, perpetuates the name of Arthur in connection with it." [209]

Here, on Ben Arthur, our Arthurian wanderings terminate; and here we may fitly review in their connection the localities we have identified as the sites of Arthur's great battles. For, thus viewed, the probable correctness of each identification will, I think, become more apparent. "According to the view I have taken," says Mr. Skene, "Arthur's course was first to advance through the Cymric country, on the west, till he came to the Glen, where he encountered his opponents. He then invades the regions about the Wall, occupied by the Saxons in the Lennox, where he defeats them in four battles. He advances along the strath of the Carron as far as Dunipace, where, on the Bonny, his fifth battle is fought; and from thence marches south through Tweeddale, or the Wood of Celyddon, fighting a battle by the way, till he comes to the valley of the Gala, or Wedale, where he defeats the Saxons of the east coast. He then proceeds to take four great fortresses:

and Rev. Godfrey) *Genealogical and Historical Sketch of the Stuarts of the House of Castle-Stuart.* The connection of our present German sovereign with the ancient line of native English and Scotish kings is of the most indirect and collateral description. On personal conduct, and popular affection, not on "right divine," is the throne now fortunately established.

[209] *Four Ancient Books,* v. I. p. 53.

first, *Kaerlium* or Dumbarton; next, Stirling, by defeating the
enemy in the *trathcu Tryweryd*, or Carse of Stirling; then *Mynyd
Agned*, or Edinburgh, the great stronghold of the Picts, here called
Cathbregion; and, lastly, Bouden Hill, in the centre of the country
between these strongholds." Twenty-one years after, is fought
at Camelon the battle of Camlan, in which both Arthur and Med-
rant perished." Mr. Skene concludes with the judicious remark,
that "in thus endeavouring to identify the localities of those events
connected with the names of Cunedda and of Arthur, I do not
mean to say that it is all to be accepted as literal history, but as
a legendary account of events which had assumed that shape as
early as the seventh century, when the text of the *Historia Britonum*
was first put together, and which are commemorated in local
tradition." [210]

Such, then, is the verification of the theory, deduced from the criticism of Cymric history, which is afforded by an exploration of the
topography of Southern Scotland and the English Border. In
the first place, we find in the Lennox, on the Firth of Forth,
and in Tweeddale, sites for all the great battles of the Arthur
of History, highly probable, to say the least, both considered
separately, and in their sequence. This only I would remark
on Mr. Skene's theory as just stated, that, as it seems to me
improbable that Arthur had Saxon foes so far west as the
Lennox, I would, on this ground, be inclined to prefer the sites
given by the writer in the *Gentleman's Magazine*, as those of his
first, and next four battles. But whether we accept Mr. Skene's
theory in its entirety, or thus modified, the fact remains that very
probable sites may be found for all Arthur's battles, not only in
Arthurian Scotland, but just in those districts of it which we know
to have formed a debateable land between Cymry, Saxons, and

[210] *Four Ancient Books*, v. I. pp. 58 and 60.

Picts during the Arthurian Age. And further, it is to be remarked that at, or in the near neighbourhood of every one of these battle-sites thus identified, we find existing, from the time of our oldest charters, and other documents, to this day, places with Arthur's name, or traditions of Arthur's history. Not far from the Glen, we have Arthur's Lee, etc. ; towering over the battle-fields on the Douglas, Ben Arthur; near the battlefield of Dunnipais (Bassas), as also near that of the final battle of Camlan, Arthur's O'on ; near the fields of battle of the Wood of Celyddon, and of Wedale, the Eildon Hills with their traditions of the departing out of this world of all the Arthurian Chivalry, and of the coming again of King Arthur; Dumbarton, where, as above, his ninth battle was fought, bears his name as Arthur's Castle; near the scene, according to Mr. Skene, of his tenth battle, we find Arthur's Round Table ; near that of his eleventh battle, Arthur's Seat ; and near his twelfth battle-field, the tradition I have above given of Cockleroy Hill. And not only are these battle-sites in the neighbourhood of traditional locali-ties, but what is, perhaps, an equally important confirmation of the correctness of these identifications, they are in the neigh-bourhood of the great Roman roads.[211] We find also, from the foregoing exploration, that the Arthurian Traditions of the various districts, in which so many historical and poetical sites of the Arthurian Age have been identified, are not only distinctively different* in each district, but that, in such difference, these traditions are in singular accordance with historical facts. In Strathmore, we have the tradition of Guenivere carried off by the Pictish Mordred ; and the fact of the country beyond the Forth having been in the possession of the Picts. Lothian and Galloway we find connected by traditions of Lothus and his son Gawayne ; and

---

[211] Compare Roy, *Military Antiquities.* One is the more struck on observing this, as Mr. Skene's identifications seem to have been made without any reference to these roads.

we know as a fact that, though separated by a wide extent of Cymric territory, these two districts were inhabited by the same Pictish race. Cumberland is distinguished by traditions of the Court of King Arthur, of which Gawayne, who is particularly mentioned as "of Scotland," "de l'Escosse," in the French Romances, is the principal hero; and Cumberland marched with his patrimony of Galloway. The Isle of Man is spoken of as inhabited by a foreign and hostile race; and it was in fact inhabited, not as the mainland by Cymry, but by Irish Scots. And so on. I do not, indeed, know of any tradition of Arthurian Scotland which, in its general features at least, is not in accordance with the results of our later historical researches.

This accordance between topographical tradition and historical fact will be further illustrated in the following chapter, in which the results will briefly be given of the later investigation of that Ossianic poetry and Fingalian tradition, which, as pointed out in Chapter II. Section (II), would have been a condition inimical to the importation into the North of Arthurian tradition, if it had elsewhere had its birthland. And, as a still further confirmation of the theory of this Essay, I shall, in the concluding chapter, more particularly show that all the chief incidents of the Arthurian Romances find in Scotland fit traditional localities, and that with "the North" are also connected all the chief characters of these Romances, with the exception, perhaps, of Sir Tristrem. From the list given in the Appendix, of Scotish Arthurian Localities, Traditional, Historical, and Poetical—a List which gives in a summary form the results of the exploration above narrated—I trust that the chief country of these localities will appear, without question, to be "the North;" and that, in this general fact, and those to which I have, in the foregoing remarks, more particularly called attention, there will be admitted to be an important inductive verification of our deductive theory that the birthland of the Traditions of King Arthur was Arthurian Scotland.

CHAPTER IV.

THE FINGALIAN RELATIONS OF ARTHURIAN LOCALITIES AS PRESENTED BY AN EXAMINATION OF PICTISH MEMORIALS.

THUS I have shewn, first, that the critical results of the examination of Cymric history, political and literary, point to what is now Southern Scotland and the English Border, as the scene of the events which were the historical bases of the Arthurian traditions; and, secondly, that the theory deduced from this historical and literary criticism has what may be justly regarded as an inductive verification in the results of the journeying narrated in the foregoing pages. And I would now proceed to point out those Fingalian relations of the Arthurian topography of Scotland which are presented by an examination of Pictish Memorials. I shall show that, as the traditions of Arthur and Merlin are what still lives for us of the Cymry of the south, the traditions of Fingal and Ossian are the still living memorials of the Picts of the north of Scotland; that Scotland beyond the northern boundary of what the localities just pointed-out suggest that we should call Arthurian Scotland, should, if it is to be similarly named from its traditional topography, be distinguished as Fingalian; and that the Cymry and Picts to whom the Arthurian and Fingalian cycles of Celtic Mythology respectively belong, were of kindred Celtic race and language, and in geographical relations to each other in Scotland similar to those which are now found to exist between the Arthurian and Fingalian topographies of that country.

SECTION (I).

The Relation of the Feinne to the Picts.

I have first, then, to show that the Fingalian traditions would appear to connect themselves with the Picts of the north, in the same manner as the Arthurian traditions are certainly derived, whether originally or not, from the Cymry of the south of Scotland. For the question as to the real position of the Ossianic poems in the literature of Scotland depends, as Mr. Skene has pointed out, on the answer to the preliminary question : " Who were the Feinne, the Fenians, or Fingalians of tradition, and to what country and period are they to be assigned ? " [1] And his investigation of this question ends in the conclusion that, whether a denomination for an entire people, or for a body of warriors, the Feinne belonged to the Cruithne, or Picts, the race prior to the Low Germans in Lochlin, or Scandinavia, and the seaboard north of the Rhine, and to the Scots in Alban, or northern Scotland, Breatan, or southern Scotland, and Erin, or Ireland. Hence, the Ossianic poems, and Fingalian traditions, appear as celebrating Pictish heroes, and recording, in a legendary form, events of early Pictish history. And hence, the Feinne, or Fenians, and the traditions which form the groundwork, at least, of the Ossianic poems, " belong to that period in the history of Scotland and Ireland before a political separation had taken place between them, when they were viewed as parts of one territory, though physically separated, and when a free, and uninterrupted intercourse took place between them." As to how the Scotish Gælic, in which these Fingalian traditions and poems have been transmitted, originated in the undalriadic parts of the Highlands ; Mr. Skene remarks that, " if the supposition be correct that the Cruithne, or Picts, spoke a Gaelic dialect, we can easily understand how, though originally different from the Gaelic dialect of Dalriada, it may, by the influence of the written language, and its vernacular use by the clergy for so long a period, have become modified, and assimilated to it."

Whether the historical events in which the Fingalian traditions originated, occurred in Alban or Erin, on the eastern, or on the

[1] *Book of the Dean of Lismore*, p. lxiv.

western side of the narrow seas dividing the ancient Pictland of the
centuries preceding the sixth, is, I would submit, a question which
can be scientifically determined only by following some such method
as that I have stated, and exemplified, in this attempt to discover
the original birthland of the Arthurian traditions.   First, there
must be deduced from the criticism of the earliest historical sources,
the time, character, and place of the events which may have been
the actual bases of these traditions; and secondly, this deduction
must be verified by the results of a thorough study of the Fingalian topography, both of Scotland and of Ireland; the assumption
being that, where there is the greatest number of Fingalian localities, there the events occurred in which Fingalian traditions originated, except such abundance of local tradition can be otherwise
more probably explained.

That, however, the Scots under whom the various Celtic and
Teutonic races of North Britain are found, at the opening of the
Mediæval age, consolidated into one predominantly Celtic nationality,
were Irish immigrants who settled in what is now Argyllshire, in
the sixth century, would appear to be certain; and that these Irish
Scots belonged originally to a southern stream of migration by
Syria, Africa, and Spain, from the Asian cradle of the Aryan race,
would appear to be not improbable.   But on the other hand, the Picts,
or Cruithne,—with whom the Fenian legends and Ossianic poetry are
by so many indications, if not positive proofs, connected,—would appear to have originally belonged to a northern stream of migration,
by Scythia and Germany, or Lochlin.   And hence, as, for the Scots
of Albany or North Britain, Erin or Ireland was the parent
country; so, for the Picts of Erin, Albany would be the colonising
fatherland.   We know, at least, as historical facts, that, as the Scots of
Albany became independent of those of Erin in 573, the Picts of
Erin threw off the yoke of those of Albany in 608.[2]   And the infer-

---

[2] See SKENE, *Chronicles of the Picts and Scots.*

ence should seem to be that it is that country which was the fatherland of the race, with heroes of which Ossianic poetry seems to be
chiefly conversant, that can best claim an original character for its
Fingalian traditions and topography.   The question at least suggests
itself, whether, in like manner, as, though all the MSS. of ancient
Cymric literature are Welsh, yet the original localities of its Arthurian poems would seem to be found in Southern Scotland ; so, though
the greater part of the MSS. of ancient Gaelic literature are Irish,
yet the original localities of its Fingalian traditions may not be
found in Western (and Northern) Scotland, rather than in Ireland ?

But whether the historical bases of the Fingalian traditions
were events which actually occurred in the third, or some later,
century ; whether the scene of these events was Albain, or Erin, or
both ; and whether, therefore, it is Scotland, or Ireland, or neither
exclusively, that was the birthland of the Fingalian traditions ;
must, for the present, be left as questions to which no definitive
answer can be given.   Certain, however, it is that Scotland has
not only an equal claim with Ireland to an Ossianic poetry[3] in
which Fingalian heroes have been "celebrated in Gaelic verse ever
since the ninth century, if not the seventh ;"[4] but that Scotland
alone can lay claim to what I would call the Fingalian Epic,
the Gaelic "Ossian," published from MacPherson's MSS. in 1807
as the original of his translation of 1762.   And this epicising
of old Ossianic fragments, for such the Gaelic "Ossian" has
now been shown to be, must be at least admitted to be a work
of very great historical importance.

---

[3] In answer to Professor O'Curry's somewhat hasty remark—" Of all MacPherson's
translations, in no single instance has a genuine *Scotish* original been found, and that
none *will* ever be found I am very certain " (*MS. Materials of Anoient Irish History*,
p. 304)—it seems here sufficient to refer to Skene's Introduction to the *Book of
the Dean of Lismore*, to the fourth volume of Campbell's *West Highland Tales*, and to
the collection of Gaelic MSS. (65 in 1862), mainly formed by Mr. Skene, and deposited
in the Library of the Faculty of Advocates.

[4] CAMPBELL, *Tales of the West Highlands*, v. IV., p. 249.

As to its literary merit, "when I read *Fingal* in the original," says one of the most competent of judges, "I feel that this is poetry, that these are grand ideas clothed in magnificent sonorous language ; on reading it in English, I often feel that there is something in it akin to bombast. . . . . . . I have no doubt that the work is founded on genuine old popular materials, and I would rank it for originality with Tennyson's *Idylls of the King*, or *Homer*, if the Greek poems were floating ballads before they were made into epic poems."[5] And our most fastidious English critic thus writes : "Its chord of penetrating passion and melancholy, its *Titanism* as we see it in Byron,[6] what other European poetry possesses that like the English, and where do we get it from ? The Celts . . . . are the prime authors of this vein of piercing regret and passion, of this Titanism in poetry. A famous book, Macpherson's *Ossian*, carried in the last century this vein like a flood of lava through Europe. . . . . Make the part of what is forged, modern, tawdry, spurious, in the book as large as you please . . . . . there will still be left a residue with the very soul of the Celtic genius in it, and which has the proud distinction of having brought this soul of the Celtic genius into contact with the genius of the nations of modern Europe, and enriched all our poetry by it. Woody Morven, and echoing Lora, and Selma with its silent halls !—we all owe them a debt of gratitude, and when we are unjust enough to forget it, may the Muse forget us !"[7]

With respect to the authorship of the Fingalian Epic, Mr. Campbell's "theory is, that about the beginning of the eighteenth century, or the end of the seventeenth, or earlier, Highland bards may have fused floating popular traditions into more complete forms, engrafting their own ideas on what they found ; and that MacPherson

[5] CAMPBELL, *Tales of the West Highlands*, v. IV. p. 155 and p. 249.

[6] On his mother's side, as will be remembered, a Scotish Gordon, and known in his boyhood at Aberdeen as Byron-Gordon.

[7] ARNOLD, *On the Study of Celtic Literature*, pp. 152-3.

found their works, translated and altered them, published the translation in 1760; made the Gaelic ready for the press; published some of it in 1763; and made away with the evidence of what he had done when he found that his conduct was blamed . . . . But till an earlier author is discovered, if such there was, MacPherson's name must be associated with his publication. And that must rank as a Scoto-Gaelic work at least a hundred years old, and till the contrary is proved, Ireland has not a ghost of a claim to it.[8]

As to MacPherson's personal character, it may not, under all the circumstances of the case, be going too far aside from our present subject to add that, though he would have had a far more desirable fame, had he " had the courage to avow the truth, and state candidly to the world how much of his work was based on original authority, and to what extent he had carried the process of adapting, interpolating, and weaving into epic poems;"[9] yet, in mitigation of our judgment, it is but fair to remember that, in his time, there was not yet that scrupulous truthfulness in antiquarian research which, but a manifestation as it is of the general increase of the scientific spirit, is characteristic of these days; and further, that the outrageous violence of the attacks led by the prejudiced, overbearing, and in this matter, utterly ignorant Saxon, Dr. Johnson,[10] was not calculated to encourage a candour which would have been certainly represented as a confession of forgery. Let us now, however,

---

[8] CAMPBELL, *West Highland Tales*, v. II. p. 80 and p. 249.

[9] SKENE, *Book of the Dean of Lismore*, Introduction, p. lii.

[10] " Here lies poor Johnson : readers have a care,
Tread lightly, lest you rouse a sleeping bear;—
Religious, moral, generous, and humane,
He was,—but self-sufficient, rude, and vain;
Illbred, and overbearing in dispute,
A Scholar, and a Christian, yet a Brute.
Would you know all his wisdom, and his folly,
His actions, sayings, mirth, and melancholy;
Boswell, and Thrale, retailers of his wit,
Will tell you how he wrote, and talked, and coughed, and spit."

forget him as the unenviable hero of the Ossian controversy, and think rather of MacPherson, whether he was, or not, in his Gaelic *Fingal*, the first to epicise the Fenian ballads, and tales of his country, yet as, in his English *Fingal*, the most considerable Scotish poet immediately preceding Burns and Scott;[11] as the Gaelic critic to whom all scholars are indebted as having been the first to waken that wide interest in Celtic researches which has already produced so much fruit;[12] and as the original genius from whom is to be dated that Celtic Revival which has already influenced, and is manifestly destined still further to influence, the political and social condition of Britain, and the literature of Europe.[13]

To sum up these remarks. We find that Scotland has, besides its Arthurian traditions, an Ossianic literature which has, through MacPherson, exercised a most important European influence; that this literature is founded on Fenian or Fingalian legends which are still current as popular tales in the West Highlands; that the Feinne, who are the heroes of these legends, belonged to the race of the Picts; that, as Scotland was the fatherland of the Picts who

[11] Mr. Skene speaks of "the wonderful tact and originality Macpherson really showed in producing his English version." *Book of Dean of Lismore*, p. liii. And Mr. Burton does not hesitate to say that "he brought to his work the true power of a great poet." *History of Scotland*, v. I. p. 179.

[12] It was the Ossian controversy that first drew attention to the ancient Welsh and Irish poems.

[13] "En présence des progrès . . . . . qui n'est d'aucune pays, et ne peut recevoir d'autre nom que celui de moderne ou européene, il serait puéril d'espérer que la race Celtique arrive dans l'avenir à une expression isolée de son originalité. Et pourtant nons sommes loin de croire que cette race ait dit son dernier mot. Après avoir usé toutes les chevaleries dévotes et mondaines, ... qui sait ce qu'elle produirait dans le domaine de l'intelligence, si elle s'enhardissait à faire son entrée dans le monde, et si elle assujettissait aux conditions de la pensée moderne sa riche et profonde nature? Il me semble que de cette combinaison sortiraient des produits fort originaux, une manière fine et discrète de prendre la vie, un mélange singulier de force et de faiblesse, de rudesse et de douceur . . . . . On se persuade qu'il est téméraire, de poser une loi aux intermittences et au réveil des races, et que la civilization moderne, qui semblait faite pour les absorber, ne serait peut-être que leur commun épanouissement."—RENAN, *La Poesie des Races Celtiques* in *Essais de Morale et de Critique*, pp. 454-6.

spread into Ireland, just as Ireland was the fatherland of the Scots who spread into Scotland, and gave it their name, it should seem not improbable that Scotland was the birthland of Fingalian, as well as of Arthurian tradition; and, finally, I would now add that the fact that the author of the Fingalian Epic was a Badenoch-man, was a native, therefore, of that Pictish province of Moray, or Moravin, which so long withstood the power of the Scotish kings, and belonged to the great clan Chattan, a tribe chiefly of Pictish origin,[14] is not a little interesting and remarkable with reference to the relation of the Feinne to the Picts.

SECTION (II).

The Relation of Fingalian to Arthurian Topography.

I have now to show that Scotland north and west of the line of the Grampians is as distinctively Fingalian in its topography, as, south and east of that line, we have found it to be Arthurian. To attempt to give anything like a complete list of the Fenian localities of Scotland would be here irrelevant. It will be sufficient for my present purpose to show that they are found more or less thickly over the whole of Scotland beyond that part of it which is distinguished by an Arthurian topography; and further, that these Fingalian localities are not found within, though some of them are on the outskirts of, the Arthurian country. Let me, then, imagine those who have accompanied me in my Arthurian journey to continue their wanderings into Fingalian Scotland.

Sailing down Loch Lomond, we find overlooking the islands at its southern end, a hill called Dun Fion, or the Fort of Fingal. Thence, through the Lennox by Glen Fruin, the "Glen of Sorrow,"

---

[14] SKENE, *History of the Highlanders.* Compare v. I. chap. IV. and v. II. chap. VI. The MacPhersons seem to have been the Clan Yha, or Clan Kay, and the MacIntoshes the Clan Quhele, whose conflict on the North Inch of Perth in 1396 is introduced with such effect in Sir Walter Scott's *Fair Maid of Perth.*

where, in the time of James VI., the MacGregors and the Colquhouns
met for the high purpose of mutual slaughter—tragic, and yet, from a
certain point of view, grimly humorous spectacle ! Then, across Loch
Long, up Loch Goil, and so, by Hell's Glen, to Inverary on Loch
Fyne. Here one might enumerate in one view a long list of Fingalian localities: Cruach-Fhinn, Innis-Chonain, Innis Aildhe, Innis
Raoine, Innis Chonnail, etc. Crossing again into Cowall we find it
" still brimful of Fenian traditions." And here, particularly, we
come on the first of those localities so tenderly commemorated in
the Lament of Deirdre over Alban, which is the foundation of
MacPherson's "Darthula," and of which there is a copy in the
Glenmasan MS. of the year 1238, now in the Advocates' Library.

> " Glendaruadh ! O Glendaruadh !
> My love each man of its inheritance,
> Sweet the voice of the cuckoo on bending bough,
> On the hill above Glendaruadh." [15]

Thence, sailing down the Kyles of Bute, and crossing the southern
end of Loch Fyne to Tarbert, we observe, in the distance, the
beautiful island of Arran, Ar-ain, or Ar-fhinn, Fin's Land, where
there is another Dun Fion. Exploring the neighbourhood of West
Loch Tarbert we remark that it is especially distinguished by its
traditions of Diarmid, the Lancelot of Arthurian Romance, and
Mordred of Arthurian Tradition. Here we find Leaba Dhiarmaid,
" the Bed of Diarmid ; " Leum na Muice, " the Swine's Leap ; " Tor
na Tuirc, " the Boar's Heap," where the boar was killed by Diarmid ;
and Sliabh Ghavil, " the Hill of Love," to which the wounded hero
is said to have addressed, as he was dying, lines still preserved by
tradition. Near this also, is Dun 'a Choin Duibh, " the Fort of the
Black Dog," which is a curious old fort in a wood, and is said to be
the place where Bran killed the black dog, as is told in a well
known ballad. Wandering up Knapdale we find, on Loch Swine

---

[15] *Book of the Dean of Lismore*, p. xxxv.

the Dun Suibhne of ballad and song. A short distance to the north, we find the site of the ancient capital of the Scotish kingdom of Dalriada, the hill fort of Dunadd, called also from its situation in the centre of the Moss of Crinan, Dunmonaidh, or "the Fort of the Moss." And thence, getting to Loch Awe, we find its shores and islands, as romantic in Fingalian legend as in natural scenery;[16] Innis Fraoch, particularly, recalling a legend wonderfully similar to that of Hercules and the garden of the Hesperides. The story is finely told by an ancient bard in a composition usually called "Bàs Fraoich," or *The Death of Fraoch*, and beginning :

> "The sigh of a friend from Fraoch's green mound,
> 'Tis the warrior's sigh from his lonely bier,
> 'Tis a sigh might grieve the manly heart,
> And might make the maid to weep."[17]

Wandering on, through the Pass of Brander, at the foot of Ben Cruachan, we come down on Loch Etive, the Loch Eitche of the Lament of Deirdre, and the Lora of the Fingalian Epic. At its southern end is Dunstaffnage Castle, more properly Dun-da-innis from two islands near it,—the Dun Lora of Ossian. The Ferry—over the rocks of which the ebb-tide thunders with deafening roar—is the Falls, and the moor on the other side is the Heath, of Lora with its dark gray stones,—the Eas Laoire, and Sliabh Eas Laoire of Mac-Pherson's Gaelic *Fingal*. Not far from this also is the Luath, another of Ossian's streams. And Dun mhic Uisneachan, now corruptly called in guidebooks, Dun MacSniachan, and also named Bail-an-righ, "the King's house or town," seems with great proba-bility identified with the Selma and Taura of Ossian, and with the Beregonium of ancient writers. Of the same Pictish, and Fingalian Uisneach, we have another record near this in Glen Uisneach. And it is to be noted that the legends of his three sons, Ainle, Ardun, and Naoise, connect them with those remarkable structures termed

---

[16] See the notes to HAMERTON'S *Loch Awe and other Poems*.
[17] *Book of the Dean of Lismore*, p. 54 and p. 36.

vitrified forts, of which Dun mhic Uisneach is one, and Dun Dhear-
dhuil, and Dun Scathaig are other examples.

Proceeding to Oban, we may take the steamer round Mull to the
sacred, but tourist-profaned Iona,[18] and to that sublime sea-cave
which bears the name of Fingal. Returning through the Sound of
Mull, we have on our left the Morvern, so often mentioned in the Fingalian Epic, but unknown in the Fingalian ballads and tales. In the
island of Liosmor, or Lismore, however, which gave its name to the
deanery of that Sir James MacGregor who, in the sixteenth century,
made the valuable collection, recently edited, of Gaelic poetry, *then*
ancient, we have more genuine Fingalian localities. Larach tigh
nam Fiann, "the Site of the Fingalians' House," is a large circular
mound of some eighty yards diameter, surrounded by a ditch, and
having near its centre a deep well which may have been used for
the purpose of entrapping game in this traditionally favourite
hunting ground of the Fingalians. And in pleasant conjunction
with these memorials of the chase is here also found Sliabh nam
Ban Fionn, "the Fingalian Fair Women's Hill." Coasting the shores
of Appin, and sailing up another of the many Lakes of Elms (Loch
Leven), we land at Ballachulish, and thence walk to Glen Coe
(Gleann Comhan), "the Narrow Glen." Here tradition fitly places
the birth-place of Ossian, "the sweet voice of Cona;" and among the
sublime precipices that wall the Glen on the east is Ossian's Cave.

Journeying up the Glen, to where it opens on the Moor of Rannoch, and turning down next day through the Black Mount Forest,
we come to Glen Orchy, another of the localities of the Lament of
Deirdre. Thence, through Glen Dochart, to Cill Fhinn, pro-
nounced in Gaelic, and written in English Killin, "Fingal's Tomb."
And in the neighbourhood we find a place called Sornach-coir-

---

[18] This island is the property of the Duke of Argyll; and one can hardly believe
that his Grace, so eminent as he is for wide culture and high feeling, can be aware of
the neglected and unguarded state in which the most ancient monuments of the Scotish
monarchy are here going to ruin. I speak from the impressions of a visit in 1866.

Fhinn, "Fingal's Oven." Proceeding up Loch Tay, we come to
the Kirkton of Fortingall, anciently the Clachan of Fothergill, where
was born that Dean of Lismore, to whose MS. of the sixteenth
century we are so much indebted. To the West of this is Glen
Lyon, the ancient Cromgleann nan Clach, or "Crooked Glen of the
Stones," associated with so many traditions of the Feinne, and where
the remains of their rude forts, termed Caistealan na Feinne, crown
many a rocky summit. And the vale is bounded on the south and
east by the heights of Drum Fhionn, or "Fingal's Ridge." Turning
again southwards, "in that awful part of Glen Almon where lofty
and impending cliffs on either hand make a solemn, and almost
perpetual gloom,"[19] is found Clachan Ossian, "the grave-stone
of Ossian;" and one of the neighbouring hills is called Monivaird,
or "the Bard's Hill." About three miles from Clach Ossian in a glen
named Corriviarlich is Fingal's Cave; and on the other side of
the Almon in Strathearn, is a small village named Fendoch, anciently
Fianntach, "Fingal's Thatch-house or Hall," where, according to the
tradition, the king came to reside after the Bail-an-Righ above
mentioned had been burned down by Garbh MacStairn.

In the Aberdeenshire Highlands, I may note, among other localities,
Bengulbain in Glen Shee, with its tradition of the famous boarhunt
of Diarmid O'Duine—

> "Then bravely did the hero of the Feinn
> Rouse from his cover on the mountain-side,
> The great old boar, him so well known in Shee,
> The greatest in the wild-boar's haunt e'er seen."[20]

Ben-Muich-Dhui is "the Hill of the Black Sow." And on the north
side of the upper valley of the Dee, in the Forest of Glen Avon,
and overlooking Inchrory, is Clach Bhean, "the Hill of the Woman's
Stone," with its legend of Fingal's wife, Grainne, the "victim," (?)
of Diarmid. Crossing the mountains here alone, early one October,

---

[19] *Poems of Ossian* (Highland Society's Edition), v. III. p. 534.
[20] *Book of the Dean of Lismore,* p. 32 and p. 22.

night fell, dark and starless, when I was still but a short way below
the sources of the Don; and I should have been lost in the snow,
but that a herd of red deer started-up from their snowy lairs, as I
came floundering in among them in the darkness, and, as they
rushed away, set a kennel of hounds, at a distance, baying in the
still night. I marked the direction of the welcome sound; and
fording the river, made straight to where it seemed to come from.

In Moray, which so long remained Pictish, is a place called Tuber
na Fein, which in an old gloss to a charter of Alexander II., of the
year 1220, still preserved in the chartulary of the Bishopric, is explained to mean "the Well of the Great or Kempis Men." Loch
Ness, near which was the Pictish capital, should seem to be named
after Naoise, the son of Uisneach, above mentioned. In Ross-shire,
there is Gleann Chonnain "Connan's vale;" and Amhain Chonnain,
"Connan's river;" and even Gleann Bhrain, in honour of Fingal's
celebrated dog, Bran. Returning southward, we find, to the south
of Loch Ness, and in Glen Roy, other Ben Gulbains, with their
traditions of

"The blue-eyed hawk that dwelt at Essaroy,"[21]

which also is in this district. And travelling westward, as we bring
these wanderings to a close, we find in Glen Elg, or Gleann Eilig,
"the Glen of the Elk," a place called Iomaire-nam-fearmor, "the
Big Men's Ridge," where tradition says that two of the Fingalians,
who were drowned in crossing Caol-reathain, are buried. Crossing
to Skye, we come into the country of Cuchullin, whom tradition connects with Dun Scathaig, another of those so-called vitrified forts.
And now, looking out on the Atlantic, we may behold such sea-
pictures as that so graphically described in the five words of the
ancient line—

"Sgaoth eunlaith air steuda saile"
A skiff of birds on steeds of brine.

"As each long Atlantic wave comes rolling in, we may see a clump

[21] *Book of the Dean of Lismore*, p. 33.

of dark razor-bills rise on the crest, and sink into the hollow trough
. . . . . riding like skiffs at anchor till fishing time comes, and
then they are up and off, to ride their steeds to battle with the
herring king." [22]

SECTION (III).

The Relation of the Picts to the Cymry.

Having thus briefly indicated the relations of the Feinne to the
Picts, and of the Fingalian to the Arthurian topography of Scotland,
we have now to point out the relations of the Picts to the Cymry in
race, language, and geographical position. From the evidence of
writers cotemporaneous with their existence as a known and distinct people; from the analysis of such remains of their language as
have come down to us; and from the inference to be drawn from
the topography of the districts which they are known to have
occupied; Mr. Skene arrives at the conclusion that the Picts were
of the Gadhaelic branch of the Celtic race; but that their language
was, to use the nomenclature by which Grimm distinguishes the
leading differences of the German dialects, a low Gadhaelic, and
hence approached in many of its forms to the low Cymric of
the Welsh; Cornish, and Armorican, or Breton, representing the
high Cymric dialects; as the Gaelic, the Irish, and the Manx, represent the high Gadhaelic dialects.

And in opposition to the popular view of the demarcation between a Cymric and a Gadhaelic population supposed to be indicated by the occurrence of the words *aber* and *inver*, Mr. Skene
shows that there were three words, *aber*, *inver*, and *conber*, ex-
pressive of the junction of one stream with another, and all formed
from the old Celtic word *ber*, signifying water; and that what we
actually find is, the Scots of the west with nothing but *invers*,
the Picts of the north with *abers* and *invers* together, and the

[22] CAMPBELL, *West Highland Tales*, v. IV., pp. 158–9.

Cymry south of the Forth and Clyde with no *abers*.[23]   Such, as far
as can be ascertained, should seem to have been the relations of the
Picts in race, and language, to the Cymry.[24]   And if this conclusion is still not free of doubt, it would now appear to be, at least
established, that the Picts belonged to the Celtic, and not, as
maintained by Pinkerton, and other eminent antiquaries of a former
generation, to the Teutonic Family.

It is but fair, however, to say that Mr. Irving, in his *History of
Scotish Poetry*, still adheres to the Teutonic theory;[25] and that Mr.
Burton, in his *History of Scotland*, expresses himself sceptically with
reference to all the solutions of the question hitherto offered ; and
points to the " close examination lately given to the vestiges of
ancient art as promising better results "—the most ancient types of
the sculptured stones being " found in the territory inhabited by the
Picts." [26]   Yet, on the whole, considering the arguments and critical
results brought forward by Robertson, MacLachlan, Skene, and
others, who appear to have far more fully investigated the subject
than either Mr. Irving or Mr. Burton, the weight of evidence appears to me, as I have said, to incline to the Celtic theory of the
race-relations of the " Painted People." But two points, which I do
not remember to have seen particularly noticed in their connection
with each other, have struck me as, at least, curious,—the accordance of the Celtic meaning of Fingalians, *White Strangers*,[27] with the
famous description by Tacitus—" Habitus corporum varii ; atque ex
eo argumenta : namque rutilæ Caledoniam habitantium comæ, magni
artus, Germanicam originem adseverant ;"[28]—and the occurrence of a

___

[23] *Four Ancient Books*, v. I. pp. 153 and 161.

[24] Compare the seventh of the ethnological propositions of Colonel Forbes-Leslie :
" The Picts were Gaels, but being pressed on by British Celts, and afterwards
augmented by British emigrants, became eventually, particularly in the eastern and
southern parts of Caledonia, not less Celtic, but to some extent British." *Early
Races of Scotland*, v. I. p. 32 *et seq.*

[25] See pp. 5–20.   [26] Vol. I. p. 202.

[27] *Book of the Dean of Lismore*, pp. 102, n.   [28] *Agricola*, xi.

" Finn " in the genealogy of Hengist and Horsa as given by Nennius.[29] And from the epithet applied to Diarmid, "Blue-eyed Hawk,"
it should seem that the Feinne continued to be a distinctively fair
race. All this, however, would only go to prove, what is otherwise
highly probable, that the northern stream of Celtic migration were a
fair-haired, and large-limbed people, and that they got in some degree
mixed with the Teutonic tribes with whom they came in contact,
and were, as it should seem, occasionally in alliance.[30] That the
Picts, therefore, were Celts, and of the Gadhaelic branch, would
appear to be the most just conclusion from our present knowledge.

The geographical relations of these two kindred Celtic races were,
in the Pre-mediæval Age, mainly determined by those eastern and
western estuaries of the Forth and the Clyde which, according
to the remark of Tacitus, almost make of the region to the north
of them a separate island. There was, however, also a Pictish
population among the Cymry of the south between Loch Ryan
and the Nith, apparently the remains of a time when Picts possessed
the whole northern half of Britain. But, though Pictish Celts beyond the Forth and Clyde, and Cymric Celts to the south of these
Firths, were thus the bases of the Scotish nationality ; there were
also two other elements, the geographical relations of which to
these two chief races of North Britain, in the Pre-mediæval Age,
must be here pointed out. Between the Cymric States of the south
and the eastern sea, was the kingdom of Bernicia with its Saxon
population extending from the Tyne, to the Firth of Forth, and
the Esk. And on the south-western side of the Dorsum Britanniæ,
the great mountain chain of Drumalban, or Backbone of Albion,
the Picts had for menacing neighbours, though of kindred Celtic

[29] C. xxxi.

[30] See as to the connection between Vecta and the Vecturiones, as one of the two
gentes of the Picts, *Four Ancient Books*, v. I. pp. 107 and 8, and compare SIMPSON
(Sir James), *On the Catstane*, etc., in *Proceedings of Soc. of Antiqs. of Scotland*, v.
IV. pp. 141 *et seq.*

blood, the small kingdom of Dalriada, founded by immigrant Scots from Ireland, and corresponding, with the exception probably of Ardnamurchan, very nearly to the modern county of Argyle. In the centre of what, in the tenth century, towards the end of this Pre-mediæval Age, is first mentioned as Scotland,[31] these four races met on a sort of neutral ground, comprising the modern counties of Stirling and Linlithgow, and occupied by a mixed population of Picts, Saxons, and Cymry. Into this debateable land the kings of the Scots also frequently carried their arms; in it lay the small districts of Calatria and Manann ; and within its limits most of the battles were fought in which the different races encountered each other in the struggle for the mastery.[32]

From the eighth to the tenth century another Teutonic element, besides that of the Lothians and the East coast, was added to the population of Scotland in the settlement on the Orkneys, and on the Western Islands and Mainland, of the Norsemen, driven to be vikings or sea-robbers,[33] by the conquests of Charlemagne, and the tyranny of Gorm, Earic, and Harald Harfager, in attempting to consolidate the petty states of Scandivania into the respective king-doms of Denmark, Sweden, and Norway.[34]　But this Teutonic element also was ultimately so completely absorbed that the most Celtic part of Scotland is now those very highlands and islands where the Norsemen were at one time supreme. It belongs to the history of the formation of the Scotish nationality, to show how the mastery

---

[31] *Supra*, p. 25, n. 14.

[32] As it was in this great plain also that Bannockburn, and the other great battles of the Mediæval, and subsequent centuries, were fought, Dean Stanley compares with it the great battle-field of Palestine, the plain of Esdraelon, or Armageddon.　*Sinai and Palestine*, p. 329, n.

[33] This name, as Robertson has shown, has no connection with *King*, being derived from *Vik*, a bay; *Viking*, a baysman.　The royal ship, authorized to destroy in lawful warfare, sailed from the *Hafn;* whilst the rover, privateer, or pirate, put off from the *Vik*, or open bay (*History of Scotland under Her Early Kings*, v. I. pp. 22, n.).

[34] Robertson, *History of Scotland*, v. I. p. 14-2.　Burton, *History of Scotland*, v. I. pp. 232 et seq.

in this war of races, this five-century-long conflict between kindred
Celts and between Celts and Teutons, was ultimately obtained
by the immigrant Celtic tribe of the Scots. But we may here
remark that though the Norsemen have been absorbed, we may
still observe traces of Scandinavian influences. For, as we have
memorials of the Picts in Fingalian, and of the Cymry in Arthurian Scotland, so, in what I may call Odinian Scotland, have we
memorials of the Norsemen. But this, not in a Norse topography,
—except occasionally such a name as Thurso,—but in Norse super-
stitions.[35] That the Teutonic mythology has left its traces only in
superstitious customs, while the Celtic mythology has its memorials
chiefly in topographical traditions, depends, partly at least, on essential differences between these two mythologies which I hope, in
another essay, to have an opportunity of pointing out. Meantime,
I cannot, without undue divergence from my present subject, do
more than note the fact that those wars of races which, throughout Europe, occupied the Pre-mediæval Age, and which ended in
France with the constitution of a Romanic, and in England of a Teutonic nationality, terminated in Scotland in the establishment of a
Celtic monarchy ;[36] and I can here only point to the important bearing of this fact on the topographical preservation in Scotland alone
of the traditions both of Fingal and of Arthur, and hence, of tales
belonging to both the great branches of Celtic Mythology.

We find, therefore, first, that Fingalian traditions connect themselves with the Picts, or, at least, with a body of warriors belonging to that race ; secondly, that the Fingalian localities of
Scotland are not only spread more or less thickly over, but are
confined to, the non-Arthurian region ; and thirdly, that the Picts,
'like the Cymry, were a Celtic race ; that, speaking generally, the
still-existing Fingalian and Arthurian divisions of Scotland coincide
with its Pre-mediæval Pictish and Cymric divisions ; that is, with

[35] BURTON, v. I. pp. 232 et seq.   [36] See above, p. 3, n. 5, and p. 27, n. 16.

its divisions as occupied by those races to whom we have traced
Fingalian and Arthurian traditions respectively.   And this limita.
tion of the Arthurian topography of Scotland to the ancient Cymric
kingdoms of the North becomes the more remarkable when we consider the apparent exceptions to the rule.   For, as we have seen, the
Arthurian localities at Alyth, at Meigle, and near Forfar,—all undoubtedly in the country of the Picts—tell us of Guenivere willingly
carried off by the Pictish king Mordred, and pursued, and punished
by Arthur.   Again we have Arthurian traditions connected with
Galloway, which was a southern Pictish province or petty kingdom.
But whom do these traditions concern but Gawayne, the son of
Loth, the Pictish king of Lothian, and the brother (or half-brother)
of Mordred ?   Do not then, such accordances between Scotish
Arthurian traditions, and Pre-mediæval historical facts prove a
further confirmation of the theory in this essay maintained, as
to the historical origin of Arthurian localities ?   Again, this
chapter will, I trust, have brought out more clearly that historical condition inimical to the importation into the North of Arthurian tradition which was but briefly alluded to in Section (II.)
of Chapter II., namely—the existence among the conquering race of
the Scots of a poetical literature and historical tradition opposed to
that of the Cymry, whose language began to die out in Scotland
with the subversion of their native Church in the eighth century.
May we not, then, in concluding this chapter, repeat, with
additional force, the question, how, except on the hypothesis of
the Arthurian traditions having originated in historical events
belonging to the Cymric kingdoms of the North, can we explain,
not merely the existence of an abundant Arthurian topography
in Scotland, but the strict limitation of that topography to the Cymric
kingdoms of the Pre-mediæval Age, and its remarkable relation to
the Fingalian topography of the ancient Pictish monarchy?   I
trust, therefore, that the Fingalian relations of Arthurian locali-

ties which I have, in this chapter, pointed-out, may be found to have
not only a general interest and suggestiveness, but to afford such a
confirmation of my theory of the origin of these localities, as to
justify the relevancy of these pages on Pictish Memorials.

CHAPTER V.

CONCLUSION—THE NEW HELLAS.

THUS the question which arose from our preliminary survey of
the Old Arthurland—namely, which of its three divisions, that of
Scotland, of England, or of France, was the birthland of Arthurian
tradition?—should seem to be definitively answered. Or, if this is
not admitted, it will, I trust, at least be granted that the number
of Arthurian localities now, for the first time, pointed-out in
Scotland, has an interest quite independent of our theory of the
origin of Arthurian traditions; and further, that the method em-
ployed in attempting to solve the problem of the historical origin of
these traditions, has the advantage of raising two perfectly definite
issues, namely—first, whether the above-stated critical results can,
in accordance with all ascertained or ascertainable facts bearing on
the subject, be maintained or not? and, secondly, whether the existence of so numerous Arthurian localities in Scotland can be otherwise
more probably explained, than on the hypothesis of the historical
Arthur having been a leader of the northern Cymry? But though
the theory above set-forth is certainly that which seems to me to
have the best and surest ground, I desire to add that, while endeavouring to state and defend this theory with all possible clearness, I
would not be understood as affirming it with any degree of unscien-
tific dogmatism. And should the only effect of this essay be to stir
up some Welsh or Breton antiquary to refute its conclusions, be it so;
let knowledge increase, and truth prevail. It will be desirable,
however, before proceeding to the main subject of this chapter—the

illustration of the unity and completeness of Scotish Arthurian Localities—to point-out the ethnological relations of Arthurian Scotland. Its geological relations will be briefly indicated in the third section.

SECTION (I.)

The Ethnological Relations of Arthurian Scotland.

First, then, in order that, at least, the prejudices of a false patriotism may not impede the acceptance of this theory of the origin of Arthurian localities, it may be well briefly to show how especially unreasonable such prejudice would, in this case, be.   From Breton antiquaries, indeed, one cannot fear that this theory will meet with a prejudiced criticism ; for not only have the Bretons, M. de la Villemarqué and M. Ernest Renan, shown themselves regardless of the petty distinctions of Celtic race, or rather tribe; but it is, if not to France, so undisputedly to writers in French,[1] that we owe the moulding of the rude Cymric traditions and legends into their European shape, as Arthurian Romances, that it can hardly be a matter of national prejudice how much, or how little, of these original legends and traditions belonged to Brittany.   But why, except, of course, on clear scientific grounds, should Welsh antiquaries, merely as Welshmen, view with disfavour a theory which makes Southern Scotland and the English Border the historical birthland of Arthurian tradition ?   That which chiefly gives this theory a reasonable foundation, is the fact of the extension of the Cymric kingdoms, in the Premediæval Age, so far beyond the limits of modern Wales, away to the Firths of Forth and Clyde.   To show, therefore, the English Border and Southern Scotland to be so rich in Arthurian localities

---

[1] The distinction is important; for two of the greatest of these writers, Walter Map and Robert de Borron, belonged to the Anglo-Norman Court of Henry II. De Borron would appear to have been an ancestor of Byron's.   See PEARSON, *Seynt Graal*, v. II. (Roxburgh Club).

as to give strong probability to the theory that, in this region of
the old Cymry-land, the Arthurian traditions originated, is thus,
surely, not to rob the Cymry of the modern Principality of anything to which even prejudice can attach itself, but, on the contrary, to add to their historic importance and renown.

And as for the Anglo-Saxon prejudice that this essay may encounter, this, of all others, is founded on mistake. The term "Anglo-
Saxon" is accurately applied to but a single early period of English
history.[2] "Anglo-Saxon," as applied to the modern British people,
and Britannic race, I believe every impartial scholar will agree with me
in thinking a gross misnomer. For if it can be shewn that there is a
large Celtic element even in the population of England itself,[3] still
more unquestionable is this, not only with regard to the population of
the British Isles generally, but also with reference to the English-
speaking peoples of America and Australasia. Even the English are
rather Anglo-Celts than Anglo-Saxons ; and still more certainly is
Anglo-Celtic a more accurate term than Anglo-Saxon, not only for
that British nationality which includes the Scots, the Irish, and the
Welsh ; but also for that Britannic race, chief elements in the formation of which have been Welsh, Scotish, and Irish immigrants. It
may, perhaps, be affirmed that this term "Anglo-Saxon" is justified,
if not by the numerical and merely quantitative, at least by the intellectual and qualitative predominance of this element in our variously
composed race and nationality. But, I venture to think, that such an
affirmation will not bear a comparison with facts. Just let one take
the trouble to reckon up for this, and the last two or three genera-
tions, the so-called "Englishmen," or "Anglo-Saxons" who have
been most distinguished, and have exercised the widest influence in
the various directions of intellectual activity, philosophical and

---

[2] See PEARSON, *History of England in the Early and Middle Ages*, v. I., in which
Anglo-Saxon has its true application in contradistinction to Anglo-Danish, and Anglo-
Norman.

[3] See NICHOLL, *Pedigree of the English*.

literary, political and military, legal and commercial. I believe that, if his list is candidly and impartially made out, he will be surprised to find how many of these " Englishmen " must be set down as, on one side, or on both, Scotsmen; how many also, Irishmen or Welshmen; and surprised to find how many even of the great Englishmen, if their ancestry is looked into, are, if not almost as much Anglo-Celts as the Scots, Irish, or Welsh, most certainly, at least, not Anglo-Saxons. It should seem time, therefore, for every one who cares for true speech—speech in accordance with the realities of things—to abandon this unhappy falsehood about Anglo-Saxons, and to speak rather of Anglo-Celts. No doubt history, particularly religious history, affords many instances of utter fictions having, for a time at least, very beneficial effects. It is needless here to give examples. But, in these days, when the chief political and social questions that occupy us are being raised by the most Celtic element in the commonwealth, it were surely well to cease using a term which is not only scientifically false, but practically pernicious. It was not wholly without reason that the old necromancers believed that there was in words a magical power.

This, however, by the way. What here more particularly concerns us is the fact that, in that district of the British Isles which I have called Arthurian Scotland, not only are all the Celtic races— Cymry, Picts, and Irish Scots—found along with Teutonic Angles in the Pre-mediæval Age; but that, afterwards, both the conquered Saxons and the conquering Normans of England were, by the policy of the Scotish kings, so freely invited and generously beneficed as settlers, that there is no district in Britain which belongs less to any one only of the various elements of the British population; and that here alone have all those elements freely met, and indistinguishably mingled. Whatever the primitive race, therefore, with which we may consider ourselves to be more particularly connected, we shall find records of our ancestors in Arthurian Scotland.

SECTION (II).

The Unity and Completeness of Scotish Arthurian Localities.

But now, one of those results of this investigation, briefly alluded to in the first chapter as giving interest to the solution of the question proposed,[4] must be more particularly noted. For whether I am right or not in the theory of Southern Scotland being the historical birthland of Arthurian tradition; to have shown how numerous are the Arthurian localities of Scotland; and to have pointed out the unique relation that here exists between Arthurian and Fingalian Topography, ought, I venture to think, to be alone sufficient to make Arthurian Scotland the classic land of those who may hereafter make use of the Arthurian Romances as the formal material of their poetic creations. And, as it will not only bring this result more clearly home to my readers, but will afford no slight confirmation to the historical theory in this Essay maintained, it will not be irrelevant to show, in conclusion, that Scotland is not only in the mere number of localities the chief country of Arthurian Tradition; but that there is a very singular unity and completeness in its Arthurian topography in reference to the various characters, tales, and incidents, of the whole cycle of Arthurian Romance.

To see, however, the unity and completeness of these traditional localities, we must first have reduced to some order the Arthurian legends and romantic tales themselves. They will, I think, be found very distinctly divisible into six classes. As either the first or last class of these legends, we may consider those which relate to the enchanted sleep, and resurrection of the Arthurian chivalry. Then we have the five classes of adventures to which, borrowing the title of the lost work of the early Scotish poet, " Huchowne of the Awle Ryale," we may give the name of " The Great Geste of Arthur."

The first class of the adventures of the " Great Geste," including the various stories of the forest life of Merlin and the young

[4] *Supra,* pp. 14 and 15.

Arthur; the loves of both master and pupil; the election of
Arthur as king; the victory of the national cause, of which he is
the representative; his marriage and the establishment of the Table
Rounde, we may conveniently distinguish under the title of the
Romance of the Forest, or the Youth of Arthur.   Then we find
in these legends and tales a great number of scenes, incidents, and
characters, which belong to all the various kinds into which the
systematic Germans have, in their treatises on æsthetics, classified
Das Komische. Of this part of the " Great Geste," at once the most
prominent and heroic character is, at least in the earlier romances,
that noble Don Giovanni, the gay knight of Galloway, the courteous
Sir Gawayne; and its most important incidents are those which
bring the " Auentyres of Arthure at the Tern Wathelyne," to a happy
conclusion in the marriage of Sir Gawayne, and the retransforma-
tion of the Foul Ladye, and the Grim Baron. This class, therefore,
of Arthurian stories may be generalized, and distinguished as the
Comedy of the Table Rounde, or the Marriage of Sir Gawayne.
Next in order may come that great class of adventures connected
with the " atchieving of the San Greal," and contained in those
romances which form a variously told epic, in which the chivalrous
and religious spirit of the Crusades had its most popular cotemporary poetic expression.   This third part of the stories of the
" Great Geste of Arthur" may, then, be distinguished as the History
of the Quest of the Holy Grail, or the Wars of Sir Perceval; for he
is ever the chief of the knights who achieve the Quest.   And under
this class may be also conveniently included those earlier legends
of the foreign victories of Arthur, of which the adventures of the
Quest afterwards took the place.   Then, as the fourth part of the
" Great Geste," we have the tragic stories of the discovery of the long
unfaithfulness of the wife, and of the friend, and the news of the
treason of the bastard son; the death of the noble, and beloved Sir
Gawayne, the wound given him by Sir Lancelot fatally re-opened in

the first battle against the revolted Mordred; the still more tragic scenes of the loveworn end of Merlin, and of the prophecies from his mystic tomb; the last parting, and soon thereafter the death of Guenivere, and of "the truest louer of a synfull man that euer loued woman; the kyndest man that ever stroke wyth swerde; the goodelyest persone that euer came among prees of knyghtes; the mekest man and the gentyllest that euer ete in halle among ladyes; and the sternest knyghte to his mortall foo that euer put spere in the reyst;"[5] and, finally, the terrible mutual slaughter of the battle by the Western Sea, "with the dolourous deth, and departyng out of thys worlde of them al." But not thus ends this wondrous Cycle of Romance. Succeeding those which may be distinguished as belonging to "the Tragedy of the Morte d'Arthur, or the Revolt of Mordred," we find a class of tales which not only give to the varied and tragic story of the "Great Geste" a high artistic repose and satisfaction, but a sort of infinite atmosphere. Such are the tales of the sore-wounded Arthur being borne away over the waves by the Ladies of Avalon to their Blessed Island in the West. And this class may be generally designated "The Vision of Avalon, or the Departing into Light."

Now what I would here point out is that the chief characters of the legends and romantic tales of all these six different classes are connected with the North; that not only are local habitations to be found in Arthurian Scotland for the chief incidents of these romances and traditions; but that these Scotish localities are all in the most natural relation to each other; in just such relation, indeed, as, had the Great Geste of Arthur been actually played out in Scotland, instead of being merely a Mediæval cycle of romantic adventures, the localities of its incidents would most probably have borne to each other; and hence, that these Romances must have had, as their bases, historical characters, adventures, and conflicts of Pre-mediæval Scotland.

[5] MALORY, *The Byrth, Lyf, and Actes of Kyng Arthur*, v. II. pp. 453–4. (Edit. SOUTHEY).

First, then, as to the persons of the Arthurian Romance-Cycle.
To Scotland alone, so far as I am aware, belong distinct traditions,
—either still living, as they for the most part are, or preserved in
legendary histories,—not only of Arthur, but of Guenivere, of Lancelot, and of Mordred; of Loth, the brother-in-law of Arthur, and of
his nephew Gawayne; of the Foul Ladye, and the Grim Baron; of
Perceval, the hero of the Quest of the Holy Grail; and, above all,
of Merlin the Wild, his twin-sister Ganieda, and his life-long love,
Viviana, the divine Lady of the Lake. And in saying this, I but
state one of the results of which the proofs have already been given
in the account of my exploration of Arthurian Scotland.

Then, as to the localities of the incidents of these Romances, observe, first, that of all the places with traditions attached to them of
the enchanted sleep of Arthur and his Knights, there seems to be
none that can, either in scenic, or traditional importance, vie with
those Eildon Hills which form the fit centre of Arthurian Scotland.
Then, as the appropriately romantic scene of the first part of the Great
Geste we have the Merlin-haunted Caledonian Forest; Arthur's Seat,
Arthur's Lee, and Arthur's Fountain; the Queen of Scotish Lakes,
Loch Lomond, or the Lake of Elms, in an island of which may
well be feigned to have arisen the enchanted Garden of Joy; the
twelve great battlefields of the Freedom-War, ending with that of
Bowden Hill; and the scenically unsurpassed Arthurian Castles of
Edinburgh, Stirling, and Dumbarton. Then, as the fit scene of the
Comedy, we have the Kingdom of Logres, with Joyeuse Garde, the
Castle of Seven Shields, Cardueil, Inglewood Forest, Castle Hewen, the
Tarn Wathelyne, the Green Chapel, and the other localities I have
noted on the English Border. The scenes of the Quest of the Holy
Grail, as of the continental conquests of Arthur, forming the third
part of the Great Geste, are, of course, beyond the limits of Arthurian
Scotland. For, where these scenes are not laid in a wholly unidenti-
fiable region, corresponding to their supernatural character, they are

generally in the sacred East, where is "the citie of Crist our the salt flude." But, with the fourth part of the Geste, we may again return to Scotland, and find fit traditional localities for the tragic incidents of the Morte d'Arthur, in the Chatel Orgueilleux; Joyeuse Garde, become again Dolorous Garde; Wedale, or the Vale of Woe; the Tomb and perennial Thorn of Merlin, where the Stream of Willows joins the Tweed in the midst of his beloved Caledonian Forest; the solitary northern Grave of Guenivere; and the sunset battle-plain of Arderydd. Finally, over the Solway, as the Great Western Lake adjoining the last fatal battle-field, may fitly rise for us the Vision of Avalon.

SECTION (III).

The Geological Relations of Arthurian Scotland.

Such is the completeness and unity of the Arthurian Topography of of Scotland, in reference to all the chief characters, and all the various classes of tales comprised in the Arthurian Romance-cycle. But not less distinctly marked, and complete in itself, is the region distinguished by this topography, both in a geological, and scenic point of view. For this Scotish district of Arthurian localities corresponds, with very singular accuracy, with two out of the four great geological divisions of the country. The first two of these are the Highlands, east and west of the Glen-more-nan-albin, the Great Glen of Albion, through which is cut the Caledonian Canal. This Highland region is separated from the rest of the country by what was anciently called the Mounth; the chain of the Grampians running from south-west to north-east, from Ben Nevis (4406 feet) to the Girdleness, the southern promontory of the Bay of Aberdeen; and having, as its central domes, Ben-muich-dhui (4300 ft.), and the surrounding Cairn-gorm Mountains, all averaging upwards of 4000 ft. It is chiefly, if not exclusively along, or within this line, prolonged to the Mull of Cantyre, that are found the localities of Fingalian Tradition. Cnt-

ting this mountain-chain at right angles, and forming the great
wind- and water-shear which separates the waters flowing into the
western sea from those running eastwards, is the other great mountain range of the Highlands, called, in Latin, *Dorsum Britanniæ* and
Dorsi Montes Britannici, and, in Gaelic, *Drum-alban,*—*Drum* being
the equivalent of the Latin *Dorsum.* It takes its rise north of 'the
isthmus, separating the Firths of Forth and Clyde, in the mountains
of which Ben Lomond is the chief ; is broken by the great moor of
Rannoch, but intersects the Mounth or Grampians at Ben Alder ;
crosses the Great Glen of Scotland at Achendrum, "the field of the
Drum," and finally loses itself in the mountains of Sutherland.[6]

The two other geological divisions of Scotland are the Midland
Valley (valley, however, only in a geological sense) and the Southern
Uplands ; the latter separated from the former by a line curiously
parallel with that of the Grampians, running, like it, from south-
west to north-east ; from Girvan in Ayrshire, to Dunbar in Had-
dingtonshire. It is these two southern geological divisions that
form, with the adjoining English border, what, characterizing it by
its traditional topography, I would call Arthurian Scotland.

Thus do we see the vast secular changes of geology connected
with, and determining such phenomena of a day as those which belong to human ages. Through millions of years worked the slow
forces of which the outcome were the present geological divisions of
Scotland. And these, at length, determined the seats of two families
of a race of men, and the localities of their distinctive traditions.

The general scenery of these two great northern and southern
divisions of Scotland is strikingly dissimilar. And yet, in this difference, there is an interesting similarity to the contrasted characteristics of the different but allied cycles of tradition and
romance, Fingalian, and Arthurian, of which the northern and
southern districts respectively are the seats. Beyond the line of

---

[6] Compare Skene, *Chronicles of the Picts and Scots,* pp. lxxxiii.-iv.

the Grampians " a sea of mountains rolls away to Cape Wrath in wave after wave of gneiss, schist, quartz rock, granite, and other crystalline masses.'"[7] And the Fingalian legends seem full of the sentiment that the rocks and caverns resounding with the Atlantic waves,—that the deep glens, and the dark mountain-lochs,—that the fleeing and pursuing shadows of the clouds on the mountain-sides, —and that, above all, the intermingling of the feminine grace and tenderness of the birch with the stately grandeur of the pine,—the intermingling of the bright and joyous music of the flashing, heather-purpling sunbeams, with the sterner, wilder voices of the storm-swept hills, would appear well-fitted to create in an imaginative and noble race.

Very different is the scenery of the southern division with the broad belt of Lower Old Red Sandstone at the base of the Grampians, the igneous rocks, and carboniferous strata of the Midland district; and the hard greywacké, shale, and limestone bands of the Silurian Uplands. Broad Firths,—Tay, Forth, and Clyde; wide, fertile plains, such as that of Strathmore between the Grampians, and the low, seaward range of the Ochils, and the Sidlaws; and abrupt, isolated crags and hills, form the chief physical features of the former district; while the latter presents us with many fountained, green-rolling, pastoral hills, breaking down into river-lighted dales, famous in story and in song. To these succeed the wild moorlands, the rich vales, and ancient forest-lands of the English border. Such, generally described, is the scenery of Arthurian Scotland. And in its more romantic, and varied, but less grand, and awe-inspiring character, it contrasts no less strongly with Scotland beyond the Grampians; than do the elaborate and worldly Arthurian Romances that find in it the fit localities of their incidents, with the primitive Fingalian traditions recalled by so many a mountain, cave, and glen, in the more northern, and wilder region.

[7] GEIKIE; *Geology and Scenery of Scotland*, p. 91.

To conclude, it is not merely to the antiquary, I venture to think, that this discussion of the origin of Arthurian localities, determination of their chief country, and indication of their Fingalian relations, may be of interest. For the new conceptions of the world, and of human history, and destiny, that science is forcing upon us, require a New Poesy for their synthetic expression; a new poesy to show that life, so far from being stripped, by the discoveries of science, of all that makes it, to the nobler sort, worth having, is, on the contrary, by the progress of scientific knowledge, invested with a new beauty, a more tragic grandeur, and inspired with a deeper sense of the environing Infinite. New conceptions require new forms for their poetic expression. And as the Italian novels of the Renaissance were a mine of poetic forms for our Elizabethan dramatists; or as, to take a more appropriate example, the old Greek legends, made an Iliad and an Odyssey of by Homer, furnished the poets of the great age of Greece with the forms of their immortal dramas; so, I believe, will the Pre-mediæval Celtic legends, as they have been prepared for us by the poetic romancers of the Mediæval Age, be found to present the most varied and easily adaptable material for the European poets who will dare unreservedly to accept Science. And, if I am right in thus thinking, then, the country in which these Pre-mediæval Celtic legends had, with such probability as may appear from the foregoing chapters, their historical origin; the country in which alone localities belonging to both the great formations of Celtic mythology have, like the shells that distinguish different but allied strata, been discovered; the country in which, particularly, the Arthurian traditions have been shown, if not indisputably to have originated, at least to have now their most numerous, and complete, their most scenically various, and romantic topographical records, will become a New Hellas.

LIST

OF

SIXTH-CENTURY LOCALITIES

IN

"THE NORTH;"

OR

THE LOCALITIES

OF

ARTHURIAN SCOTLAND.

NOTE.—These Localities are distinguished as Traditional; Historical,—chiefly occurring in *Nennius;* and Poetical,—for the most part found in the *Four Ancient Books.* The testimonies to the age of the Traditional Localities, the references to the original sources for the Historical and Poetical Localities, and the authorities for the identifications of Localities of these two latter classes, are given at full in the third chapter. And the Localities will be found in that chapter under the same heads, and in much the same order as they are here given.

EASTERN DIVISION.

DISTRICT I.—STRATHMORE.

MORDRED'S CASTLE	Fort on Barry Hill, near Alyth.
GANORE'S GRAVE	In Churchyard of Meigle.
STONE OF ARTHUR	
ARTHURSTONE	In Parish of Cupar Angus.
ARTHUR'S FOLD	
ARTHUR'S SEAT	Rock on Dunbarrow Hill.
TAWY	The Tay.
BENOIO	Albanak, or Albany.

DISTRICT II.—FIRTH-OF-FORTH.

FRENESSICUM, OR FRISICUM MARE .	The Firth of Forth.
FRISICUM LITUS	North shore of Firth.
CULROSS	Monastery on North shore.
GWRUID OR WERID	The Forth.
TRATHEU TRYWRUID.	Links of Forth, or Carse of Stirling.
SNOWDON WEST CASTLE	Castle of Stirling.
KING'S KNOT, OR ARTHUR'S ROUND TABLE	Under Stirling Castle.
ARTHUR'S O'ON (OVEN)	Near Larbert.
CAERE, OR CARUN	The Carron.
RYD AT TARADYR	The Ford of Torrator on the Carron.
BASSAS	Dunipais (Dunipace).
CAMLAN	Camelon, near Falkirk.
CATRAETH, GALTRAETH, OR CALATHROS	Calatria.—East end of Stirlingshire.
HAEFE, OR AERON	The Avon.
CAIRPRE	Carriber.
MANAN, OR CAMPUS MANAND . .	Slamannan Moor.
LODONEIS	Lothian.
GODODIN	North part of Lothian.
BODGAD, OR BADCAT	Bathgate.
KALDRA	Calder Water.
MONS BADONIS	Bowden Hill.
LECHLLEUTU	Linlithgow.
AGATHES	Irongath Hill.
CAER EIDDYN	Caredin.
PENGUAL, PEANFAHEL, PENNELTON, OR CENAIL, ...	Town at east end of W. of Antonine.
YNYS EIDDYN	Blackness.
ABERCOURNIG	Abercorn.
CAER GOVANNON	Dalmeny.
CAER VANDWY, OR CAER AMON . .	Cramond.
CAER SIDI, URBS GIUDI, OR JUDEU ?	Island in Firth of Forth—Inchkeith (?).
MYNYD AGNED, OR DUNEDIN . .	
CASTRUM PUELLARUM, OR CASTLE OF MAIDENS	Edinburgh Castle.
DOLOROUS VALLEY	

GRAVE OF VECTA (?)	The Cat-stane, Kirkliston.
ARTHUR'S SEAT	At Edinburgh.
DUNPELEDUR, OR DUNPENDER LAW.	Trapender Law, near Haddington.
DUBGLAS	Dunglas (?).
BASSAS	Bass (?).
KEPDUFF	Kilduff.
ABERLEFDI	Aberlady Bay.
THE BUSH OF MAW	The Moss of Maw.

DISTRICT III.—TWEEDDALE.

GWAEDOL, WEDALE, OR VALLIS DOLORIS . . . . GWENYSTRAD, OR THE WHITE STRATH	} Vale of Gala.
CASTLE GUINNION, OR GARANWYNYON	Roman Fort on Gala Water.
CHURCH OF S. MARY	At Stowe.
WHITE STONE OF GALYSTEM . . .	Near the Lady's Well at Stowe.
TYWI	The Tweed.
S. MUNGO'S WELL	At Peebles.
NEMUS CALEDONIS, OR COED CELYD-DON	} Caledonian Forest.
MERLIN'S GRAVE	At Drummelzier.
TEIFI	The Teviot.
DIN GUORTIGERN	On the Teviot.
TOMB OF ARTHUR AND HIS KNIGHTS	Under the Eildons.
DIN DREI, URBS GIUDI, OR JUDEU .	On the Eildon Hills (?)
CATRAETH	Near the Eildons (?).
MELROS	Melrose.
RHYMER'S GLEN . . . . HUNTLY BURN	} At Abbotsford.
RHYMER'S TOWER	At Earlston on Leader Water.
CALCHVYNYD, OR CALCHOW . . .	Kelso.
ATBRET JUDEU AND JUDEU (?) . .	Near Jedburgh (?).
GODODIN	District about Jedburgh (?)
GLENI, OR GLEIN (?)	The Glen—Tributary of the Till.
ABERWICK, OR JOYEUSE GARDE .	Berwick.

SOUTHERN DIVISION.

DISTRICT IV.—NORTHUMBERLAND.

NORTHOMBELLANDE	Northumberland.
BERNEICH AND TER BRENECH . .	Berenicia, or Valentia.
LLEU	The Low.
MEDGAUD INSULA	Holy Island, or Lindisfarne.
DINGUAYRDI, DINGUAROY, GUURTH-BERNEICH, BEBBANBURGH, OR CHATEL ORGUEILLEUX	Bamborough.
ARTHUR'S HILL	At Newcastle.
SEWING SHIELDS CASTLE . . . KING'S AND QUEEN'S CRAGS . . . ARTHUR'S CHAIR . . . . CUMMING'S CROSS.	On the Roman Wall near Housesteads.
DAGSESTAN	Dawston.

DISTRICT V.—CUMBERLAND.

ARTHUR'S HILL	In Liddesdale.
CAER GWENDDOLEW	Moat or Strength of Liddel, near the village and burn of Carwhinelow.
ERYDON	Ridding, near above fort.
ARDERYDD	Arthuret
CAER LLIWELYDD, OR CARDUEIL .	Carlisle.
GUASMORIC	Near Carlisle (Palmecastre, or Walmeceastre).
EDEN	Same name still.
INGLEWOOD FOREST	Ditto.
TARN WATHELYNE	Tarn Wadling.
CASTLE HEWIN	Near Upper Hesket.
BARON-WOOD	On the Eden.
HATTON HALL . . . . PLUMPTON PARK	Same name still.
ARTHUR'S ROUND TABLE	Near Penrith.
BROUGHAM CASTLE	
GWENSTERI	The Winster
DERWENNYD.	The Derwent.
VOLSTY CASTLE	
THE GRENE CHAPEL	Chapel of the Green.
MANAU, OR EUBONIA	Isle of Man.

DISTRICT VI.—GALLOWAY.

GALWADIÆ MARE.	Solway Firth.
GALWYDDEL.	Galloway.
HODDELM	Hoddam.
CHURCH OF S. MUNGO	In Presbytery of same name.
MABON	Nithsdale and Lochmaben.
MAN-LLACHAR.	Lochar Moss.
CLUDVEIN, OR CLEDYFEIN	The Cluden.
GARANT	The Carron—Tributary of the Nith.
CAER RYWC	Sanquhar on the Crawick.
CUTHBRICTISKCHIRCH	Kirkcudbright.
GRAVE OF GWALLAWG AP LLEENAWG	King Galdus's Tomb.
KIRKGAWAYNE ?	Kirkcowan.
MARSH OF TERRA.	Glenterra.
CAER RHEON	Cairnryan.
LLWCH RHEON	Loch Ryan.
RHYD RHEON	Ford of Ryan.
NOVANT	Mull of Galloway.

WESTERN DIVISION.

DISTRICT VII.—AYR.

CARRAWG	Carrick.
COEL	Kyle.
CANOWAN	Cunningham.
DINDYWYDD	Dunduff.
DYVNWYDD.	A District of Ayr.
GRAVE OF CARADAWG	Tomb of Caractacus.
CAER CARADAWG.	Caractonium.
GAFRAN	Girvan.
GRAVE OF COEL	Tomb of King Cole at Coilsfield.
CRAGS OF KYLE	
BURN OF COYL.	Near town of Ayr.
PARISH OF COYLTON	
BRETRWYN	Promontory of Troon.
DUNDEVENEL	Dundonald.
GLENI OR GLEIN	The Glen—Tributary of the Irvine.
WOOD OF BEIT	Moor of Beith.

DISTRICT VIII.—STRATHCLYDE.

CLUD	The Clyde.
MERLIN'S FOUNTAIN	Sources of Clyde (?).
ARTHUR'S FOUNTAIN	In parish of Crawford.
ARFYNYDD	Upper Strathclyde..
LLANERCH	Lanark.
GODEU	Caidzow–Middle ward of Lanarkshire.
CALATERIUM NEMUS.	Calderwood.
REGIO LINTHEAMUS, OR LINTHCAMUS	Cambuslang.
MOUNTAIN OF BANNAWC	Cathkin Hills in p. of Carmunnock.
ARECLUTA	Strathgryfe, or Renfrewshire.
ARTHUR'S LEE.	
LOW ARTHUR'S LEE.	In Neilston Parish.
WEST ARTHUR'S LEE	
CAER CLUD, OR PENRYN WLETH .	Glasgow.
MONS GWLETH.	Dew, or Dowhill, at Glasgow.
S. MUNGO'S WELL	In Cathedral of Glasgow.

DISTRICT IX.—LENNOX.

MUREIFF.	North side of Roman Wall, or Mur.
REGED.	The same, including Loch Lomond.
ARGOED LLWYFAIN	District about Ben Lomond.
DINRIDDWG	Mugdock.
ARDUNNION.	Ardinny.
DRUM ESSYD	Kilsyth Hills.
HEIGHT OF ADOYN	Cliff on western brow of Fintry Hills.
NEMHTUR, OR NEVTUR.	
CATHRAIG IN LEOMHAN	
URBS LEOGIS, OR LEGIONIS . . .	
KAERLIUM, OR KAERLION	Dumbarton.
ALCLYDE, OR PETRA CLOITHE . .	
CASTRUM ARTHURI, OR ARTHUR'S CASTLE.	
LEUM, LEAMHUIN, OR LEAMHAN .	The Leven.
STAGNUM LIVAN, LUMUNOY, OR LIMONIUM, LLWCH LLIVANAD .	Loch Lomond.
LEAMHANACH, LEVENACHS, LLWY-FENYDD, OR LINNUIS	Lennox, to west of L. Lomond.
DUBGLAS	The Douglas.
BEN ARTHUR	At head of Loch Long.

NOTE

ON THE ARGUMENT FOR ARTHUR AS A WEST-OF-ENGLAND KING.

PROOFS of the foregoing Essay having been forwarded by Mr. Furnivall to Mr. Pearson, the learned author of the *History of England in the Early and Middle Ages*, a discussion took place between him and myself, at the close of which I requested him to give me a memorandum of the chief points in his case, in order that the question as to the Historical Origin of Arthurian Localities generally, and as to the locality of Arthur's exploits in particular, might be presented with the utmost possible fairness and completeness to those who might be interested in the subject. This he has very courteously, and obligingly done. And my readers will thus have an opportunity of judging for themselves whether the established theory, which could not, I believe, have any more able and learned defender than Mr. Pearson, or the new theory, advocated by Mr. Skene and myself, rests on the better evidence.

But before presenting his note, I would offer a few remarks on its general bearing in reference to the theory in the foregoing Essay maintained. And in the first place, I would observe that his argument touches only a small part of that general theory. For I have endeavoured to show not merely that, of the three regions of the traditional Arthur-land—Southern Scotland, Western England, and North-Western France— the historical Arthur, or the Arthur of Nennius, belonged to the first-mentioned; but also, that, of a large proportion, at least, of the ancient historical poems of the Cymry, the scenery and events belong to Southern Scotland, with which likewise are connected the warriors celebrated in these poems, and the bards who sing their praises; further, not only that personages, more or less directly and intimately connected with the Arthurian story, such, for instance, as Merlin and Kentigern, historically belong to the South of Scotland, and to the Arthurian Age; but that all the chief characters of the Arthurian Romances are to be found, in a topographically preserved and still living tradition, in what I have called Arthurian Scotland, and, as far as I am aware, in that region alone; and finally, that these topographical records and traditional tales are in the most striking accordance with historical facts.

Now, whatever objections may be urged by Mr. Pearson or others against a theory which places Arthur as an historical personage in the North, I have but little fear that any competent scholar will be found prepared to deny that these ancient Cymric poems do for the most part belong to Arthurian Scotland; that to the same region the historical Merlin belonged; that there also are to be found a greater number and variety of Arthurian traditions than in any other region of the Old Arthur-land; and that such traditions have there more remarkable historical correspondences than are anywhere else to be discovered. But if such facts as these cannot be denied; then, I think, that what appears to be the legitimate inference from them must be accepted;—namely, that it was in actual characters, incidents, and conflicts of the Pre-mediæval History of Scotland that the traditions, topographically preserved in Arthurian Localities, originated; and that in such actual characters, incidents, and conflicts, the historic element of the Arthurian Romances of Mediæval European Literature is to be found. This, however, is all that I am concerned to maintain. But let us see what Mr. Pearson can say in favour of the hypothesis that Arthur was not a leader of the Cymry of Southern Scotland, but a petty king of Western England.

Most singular, I will only remark, it would be if, in conjunction with such facts as the above, such an hypothesis should force itself upon us.

"There seem to me to be fairly good reasons for referring Arthur to a district in the South or West of England, in spite of the fact that Scotland is distinctly richer in Arthurian localities. The one historical event with which we can almost certainly connect his name is the battle of Mons Badonicus; and this is referred by Gildas to the year 520,[1] when we have reason to think that the West Saxons were beginning to press on the Britons of Somersetshire and Wiltshire, whereas the wars of Ida in the North with the Kymri of the Western Lowlands are ascribed to a later period (A.D. 547) by our earliest notices.[2] The tradition commemorated in the *Vita Gildæ*, that Arthur, King of Cornwall and Devonia, was at war with Melvas of Somersetshire, points to a district in the South; and if Melvas be indeed the Maglocunus, or Maelgoun of Gwynedd, whom Gildas speaks of as making war on his uncle, contracting an unlawful marriage, and turning monk, his resemblance to the Lancelot of romance becomes very great.[3] After Gildas our first authority for Arthur's history is Nennius. Now the English Nennius (who was certainly not ignorant of Cumbrian history, as he gives us most valuable details about Ida and Urien), says, if we take his words literally, that Arthur led the kings of the Britons in their wars against the kings of the Cantii.[4] It is true that the passage may be explained to mean that he led them against the Saxons; but even if we adopt this rendering, it is surely more natural to apply the term "Saxons" to the people strictly so called at the time when Nennius wrote (West Saxons, South Saxons, etc.), than to

---

[1] WENDOVER, I. p. 64. GILDAS; Pref. by STEVENSON, p. ix.

[2] *A. S. Chron.* A. 547. *Sim. Dun. Præfatio.*

[3] *Vita S. Gildæ*, c. 10.. *Epistola Gildæ*, c. c. 33-35.

[4] NENNIUS, c. 56. I have not taken into account the marginal note to one observation of Nennius, which places Bregnion, the scene of one of Arthur's battles in Somersetshire, or the marginal gloss on Gildas, which says that Mount Badon was near the mouth of the Severn. But they are at least evidence of concurrent traditions.

assume that it refers to a colony of their ancestors, seated for a time in Northumbria.[5] Moreover, the death-song of Geraint connects that hero, who was of Dyvnaint or Devonia, with Arthur.[6] These notices one and all, therefore, refer Arthur to a district in the South and West; while none that I know of takes him into the North till the times of Geoffrey of Monmouth.

[5] Mr. Glennie informs me, on Mr. Skene's authority, that the Cambridge MS. of Nennius reads " Tunc Arthur pugnabat contra illos, videlicet Saxones." The question, then, is whether or not "Saxones" can be referred to Angles north· of the Humber, or to a Saxon colony that preceded the Angles in those parts. To myself the words of Nennius seem distinctly to imply that he was thinking of the South of England. Throughout the Historia Britonum he uses the word Saxons (taken alone) in its special sense, and calls the people against whom Dutigirn fought (c. 62) Angles, the people whom Ecgfrith ruled "Saxones ambronum" (c.57), and Edwin's subjects "ambrones" simply (c. 63). "Ambrones" I take to be a corrupt form of Bede's word "Hymbronenses" (H. E. IV. c. 17) Humbrians, and its use with "Saxones" seems to me to imply that Nennius did not like to speak of Northumbrians generally as Saxons without qualification. Gildas uses the name Saxons for the people who fought against Vortigern and Aurelius Ambrosius, but seems not to know the name Angles. Bede speaks more than once of "Anglorum sive Saxonum" as if they were convertible terms (H. E. I. c. 15, V. c. 9), and applies either name to the people of Kent (whom he knows more precisely as Jutes), and sometimes seems to speak of the Germanic conquerors of Britain generally as Angles. But he never, so far as I am aware, uses the term Saxons in speaking of Northumbrians, or as a general name like Angli. An examination of the Codex Diplomaticus has shown me two cases in which the term Angli is perhaps used generally for Englishmen before the reign of Alfred. Under Alfred and Edward the Elder, the term "Anglo-Saxon" seems to be that most favoured. Afterwards the use of "Anglus" prevails. But I know of no instance in any Anglo-Saxon charter or author in which the name Saxon is applied to Englishmen of the North. It is true the practice of Keltic writers is not equally invariable. The Gododin poems twice designate the enemy against whom the British chiefs engaged, have fought, or are fighting, as Saxons; and probably refer in both cases to the Germanic population of Northumbria. It is true, too, as Mr. Glennie has pointed out to me, that Nennius must have thought of Ochtha and Ebissa, the son or nephew of Hengest, who, he says (c. 38), occupied country up to the confines of the Picts, as Saxons in the strictest sense. But I do not think these exceptions can outweigh the general consent on the other side, or the indications derived from the language of Nennius, when he connects the rise of the Saxons with Ochtha's emigration southward, and the history of the ·kingdom of Kent. I may add that, as far as I can discover, Nennius never applies the name " Brittones" to the Keltic peoples North of Solway, in the fifth century.

[6] SKENE, *Four Ancient Books*, v. I. p. 267. I may add, that whether Llongborth be the Longport of Kent, the Langport of Somersetshire, or merely a port on the coast, it seems to point to an attack by sea which might easily be made in South England, but not, I think, in Scotland. It is noticeable, too, that Geraint was a Devonian name. *Aldelmi Opera*, p. 83.

"Looking now to mere probabilities, I find that Cornwall, Devonshire, and parts of Wiltshire and Somersetshire, maintained their independence till the time of Ine.[7]   I find that a principality composed of Somersetshire and part of Wiltshire, of Gloucestershire and Worcestershire, of Hereford and Monmouth, defended by Selwood Forest, by the Cotswold Woods, by Wire Forest, and by the Somersetshire marshes, had its own dynasty of chiefs before the Romans,[8] and a metropolitan city for a native church at Caerleon in the sixth century.[9]   A sovereign of this country with a certain federal supremacy over Devonshire and Cornwall in the South, and Powys and Gwynedd in the North, would come into collision with the Saxons along the marshes of Wiltshire, and the line of the Severn, and with the people of South Wales (whether Gaelic or Kymric at that time) in Glamorganshire.[10]   In these districts may be found localities that correspond pretty exactly to the names of Arthur's battles as given by Nennius.[11]

"Take now the evidence of legend. In the Breton traditions collected by Geoffrey of Monmouth, Arthur is born at Tintagel, crowned first in Silchester by Dubricius, Archbishop of Caerleon on Usk, and afterwards more solemnly at Caerleon, and dies in Cornwall, and is buried in the Isle of Avalon. Even the Metrical Boece, which transfers the battle of Camlan to the Humber, steadily represents Arthur as King of South Britain. William of Malmesbury, whose *Liber de Antiq. Glaston. Ecc.* was written about the middle of the twelfth century, gives a legend from the gests of

---

[7] GUEST, *On the Boundaries of the Welsh and English Races. Archæological Journal*, xvi. pp. 105-132.

[8] AKERMAN, *On the Condition of Britain, Archæologia*, xxxiii. p. 177.   GODWIN'S *Archæologist's Manual*, pp. 16, 17.

[9] ROWLAND WILLIAMS, *On the supposed reluctance of the West British Church to convert the Anglo-Saxons. Archæologica Camb.* Oct. 1858. Mr. Stevenson thinks that Gloucester and Somerset were two of the dioceses. BEDE, *Hist. Ecc.* p. 100, note.

[10] "A line drawn from Conway on the north to Swansea on the south would separate the two races of the Gwyddyl, and the Cymry on the west and on the east." SKENE, *Four Ancient Books*, v. I. p. 43.

[11] E.g. I should place the four battles in "regione Linnuis" in the district of the Llyfni (Glamorganshire); that at Bassas near Baschurch, in Shropshire; that of Urbs Legionis at Caerleon on Usk, and that of Mount Badon at Bath.

King Arthur, which does not exist in Geoffrey of Monmouth, and which speaks of him as holding court at "Karlium," and visiting Glastonbury. William also says that Arthur gave lands to Glastonbury, and was buried there with his wife between two pyramids.[12] As the historian does not speak of the disinterment of Arthur's body, he probably wrote before it took place in 1166;[13] and this is the more likely, as he was born in the preceding century. He is, therefore, independent evidence to a tradition slightly anterior to the search made, and probably anterior to the history of Geoffrey of Monmouth, the last six books of which were not published before 1147. The search for Arthur's remains has been twice described by Giraldus Canbrensis, in the *De Instructione Principum*,[13] and in the *Speculum Ecclesiæ*.[14] The latter and fuller account, which refers with some contempt to the "fabulosi Britones," who made Morgan a fairy, is written with a minuteness which seems to me incompatible with wanton lying. Both narratives are posterior to Henry the Second's time, and therefore were not written to support his policy. Both dwell upon the fact that Guenever's hair crumbled into dust when it was exposed to the air. Clearly the Glastonbury monks could not have forged evidence of this kind. The most that can be said is that they may have fabricated the inscription found on the coffin. Even this would have been highly hazardous, as they could scarcely tell before-hand that an unopened tomb contained two bodies, one of them a woman's.

"Why, then, are Arthurian localities comparatively rare in the district where Arthur lived and reigned? Simply, I think, because from its natural wealth, it was the object of incessant attack from the Saxons, and was conquered and partially peopled anew at an early period by a people who had no interest in perpetuating the memory of their old antagonist. It is easy to see how the story

[12] GALE, iii. pp. 306, 307, 326.

[13] BROMPTON, c. ii. 52. It is remarkable that Malmesbury dedicates his book to a Henry, Bishop of Lincoln, who cannot be identified, unless the title be a clerical error for Henry, Bishop of Winchester; and that Giraldus speaks of the search as made by Henry, afterwards Bishop of Worcester, who does not appear on any extant list of Bishops.

[14] *De Jur. Prin.*, pp. 191-193. *Speculum Ecclesiæ*, pp. 47-49.

of Arthur would be carried into Brittany by fugitives before Ine.
It is more difficult, I admit, to explain how it travelled North. But
it is possible that Cadwallon recruited Britons from Devonia in the
long and prosperous wars which he waged against the Northumbrian
kings. 'Those immense forces, which nothing could resist,'[15] were
surely not drawn altogether from North Wales ; and it was a time
of peace in the South, when it could well spare soldiers."

The foregoing very learned note of Mr. Pearson's contains, I believe,
all that can be said in favour of Arthur as a West of England king.
It will be found, however, that the supports of his theory are essen-
tially but three in number—Gildas, Nennius, and the Mediæval writers.
Let us examine the two first; the last we shall find it unnecessary
specially to consider. First, as to Gildas, we must distinguish between
the *History* by Gildas, and the *Life* of Gildas. The former alone is Pre-
mediæval, and of an authority independent of those Mediæval legends,
the truth of which we are seeking to investigate. Now the *History*
gives us no certain indication whatever as to the site of the *Mons Badonicus* of Arthur's twelfth battle. For the expression, "qui prope Sabri-
num ostium habetur," is an interpolation of the Durham MS. of the
thirteenth century. As to the *Vita Sancti Gildæ*, as it is not older
than the twelfth century, it must rank, as an authority, with Geoffroy
of Monmouth, and the other Mediæval writers. And what credence
we should give to them must depend on their accordance with the
other earlier historical authority which we now proceed to examine.

Secondly, then, as to Nennius, Mr. Pearson's argument is here twofold.
In the first place he says that the *illos* against whom Arthur fought
were the *reges Cantiorum*.[16] And, secondly, that if we are to understand Nennius as meaning that he fought against the Saxons, then it
must have been in the south, because the Teutonic invaders were in
the north called Angles. As to the first argument, without pausing to
remark that it would take Arthur from the south-*west* of England,

---

[15] BEDE, *Hist. Ecc. Lib.* iii. c. 1.   [16] NENNIUS, § 56, p. 47 (English Hist. Soc.).

where Mr. Pearson places him, to the south-*east*; it appears enough to
say that, the whole passage being read, the sentence about the *reges
Cantiorum* is, or, to say the least, may be meant as merely parenthetical; while the "illos, videlicet Saxones," of the Cambridge MS.
seems to settle the matter. There remains, then, but the second argument, namely that "Saxones" is applied only to the Teutonic settlers of
the south of England. But remark, first, that Nennius *does* apply this
term to the northern invaders. For he says that the son and brother
of Hengest, and their followers, certainly as much "Saxones" as
Hengest himself and his followers, occupied the "regiones quæ sunt in
aquilone; juxta murum, qui vocatur Guaul."[17] And this being so,
remark, secondly, that Nennius could not consistently have called the
northern invaders Angles or anything else but Saxons. Again, remark, thirdly, how very naturally that parenthetical sentence about
the *reges Cantiorum* comes in, if we understand Nennius to mean that
Arthur's successes were against the northern Saxons. Hengest being
dead, Octa, his son, came from the north to take his place in Kent;
"tunc Arthur pugnabat, etc;"[18] then Arthur fought against the
northern Saxons, and, their great leader having thus left them, the
fortune of war turned in favour of the Cymry. But the main thing
to be remarked here is, fourthly, that Nennius *could not* have called
the Northern invaders Angles, because their first settlement in Bernicia was considerably later than the time he is speaking of, namely
in 547, under Ida. And, fifthly, this becomes still further clear when
we find that the earlier Teutonic settlers in the North were *Frisians*,
a tribe of *Saxons*, who could not have been referred to as Angles.[19]

Thus it seems clear that, to say the very least, there is as little in
the history of Nennius as in that of Gildas which can be held to fix
the locality of the historical Arthur in the south. But it will, I
think, seem also clear that when two such scholars and critics as Mr.

---

[17] NENNIUS, § 38, p. 29 (English Hist. Soc.)   [18] Ibid. § 56, p. 47.
[19] SKENE, *Early Frisian Settlements in Scotland*; and SIMPSON (Sir James) *On
the Catstane at Kirkliston*, etc., in *Proceedings of the Soc. of Antiqs. of Scotland*, v. IV.

Pearson and Mr. Skene can take diametrically opposite views as to the meaning of Nennius, who is really our only important authority, the question must, if it is to receive a definitive answer, be treated after some new method. "If not Gildas," says Mr. Pearson, "certainly Nennius may be understood as placing Arthur in the south; in the south may be found localities with names more or less nearly corresponding with those of his twelve battles; and, though the Mediæval histories may have no authority by themselves, yet in confirmation of this view of the meaning of Nennius, they are certainly of weight." Mr. Skene, on the other hand, maintains not only that the historic Arthur is the Arthur of Nennius, in which, I suppose, Mr. Pearson would agree with him, but that Nennius places him in the North; that in the North the sites of his battles may be identified; that the mythic Arthur is the Arthur of Geoffrey, the writers of the twelfth century, and their followers; that his story was introduced from Bretagne by Rhys ap Tewdwr in 1077, when the scene of his exploits was removed to the South; and hence, finally, that quotations from the writers of the twelfth and subsequent centuries cannot be considered as having any logical bearing on the question.

It is in reference to this state of the discussion, that the method I have followed in the foregoing Essay may, perhaps, be held to be no immaterial contribution to the settlement of the point in dispute. That method consisted, as will be remembered, first, in examining Cymric history for a deduction as to the birthland of Arthurian Tradition; secondly, in verifying this deduction by shewing that the region thus indicated is the chief country of traditional Arthurian localities; and, thirdly, in investigating the relations of this topography. It may, indeed, be said with reference to what I have specified as conditions inimical to the importation of Arthurian traditions into the North; as direct indications of the North as the birthland of these traditions; and as conditions favourable to the importation of such traditions, into the South—that our knowledge of the period is but limited. Such a reply, however, implicitly admits all that I affirm, namely, that, as far as our present knowledge goes, Cymric history points to the North rather than to the South as the country of the historical Arthur. And whatever may be said in answer to this critical deduction, I venture to think that in the very great number of indisputably ancient traditional localities, and of, at least, highly probable historical, and poetical identifications here collected, there will be found a body of facts of which the only satisfactory explanation must be found in some such theory as that in this Essay maintained.

And I say this with the more confidence, as my general result as to Arthur would appear to be in accordance with that of my collaborateur, Mr. Nash, with respect to Merlin. Mr. Nash shows that, in the Merlin of Romance, three persons are confounded, and that the really historical Merlin was a bard of the North, in the sixth century. So, I would suggest, as I have, indeed, already hinted [CH. II. (S. III).], that in the Arthur of Romance there are confounded more persons than one, though the Arthur to whom, as an actual historical character, the traditions of the great conquering king are ultimately to be traced, was simply a sixth-century *Guledig*, or Leader of the Northern Cymry. And thus, I should hope that even Mr. Pearson, and those who think with him, may find it possible to reconcile their particular theory as to Arthur with the acceptance of the more general theory which I have sought to establish with respect to the historical origin of Arthurian Localities. With whatever modifications that theory may be held, there will, I trust, be found reasons advanced in the foregoing Essay sufficient to support the general conclusion that the chief historical basis of the Mediæval Arthurian Romances is revealed to us in the Pre-mediæval history of that region which I have distinguished as Arthurian Scotland.

STEPHEN AUSTIN, PRINTER, HERTFORD.

Also published by Llanerch:

ARTHUR AND THE BRITONS IN WALES AND
SCOTLAND by W. F. Skene, edited by Derek Bryce
and based on extracts from *The Four Ancient Books.*

JOHN OF FORDUN'S CHRONICLE OF THE SCOTTISH
NATION, edited by W. F. Skene.

FOLKLORE OF SCOTTISH LOCHS AND SPRINGS
by James M. Macinlay.

LIVES OF THE SCOTTISH SAINTS
translated by W. Metcalfe.

TALIESIN POEMS
translated by Meirion Pennar.

THE BLACK BOOK OF CARMARTHEN
selected translations by M. Pennar, including
the Merlin Verses said to have been composed
in the Caledonian Forest.

SCULPTURED MONUMENTS IN IONA
AND THE WEST HIGHLANDS
by James Drummond.

THE TOMBS OF THE KINGS:
AN IONA BOOK OF THE DEAD
by John Marsden.

THE ROMANCES AND PROPHECIES OF
THOMAS OF ERCELDOUNE (THOMAS RHYMER).
edited by J. A. Murray.

For a complete list of 100+ titles, write to Llanerch
Publishers, Felinfach, Lampeter, Dyfed, SA48 8PJ.

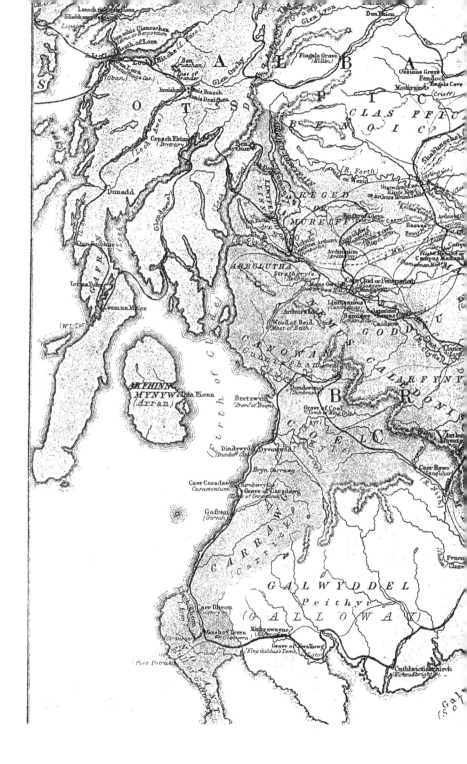

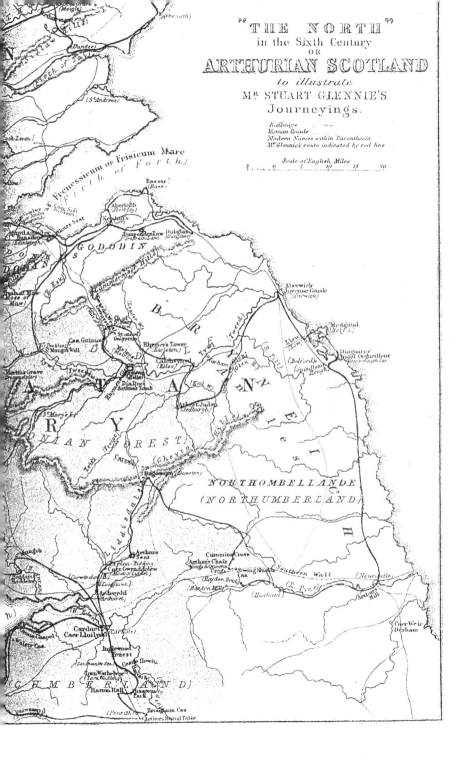

"THE NORTH"
in the Sixth Century
OR
ARTHURIAN SCOTLAND
to illustrate
Mr STUART GLENNIE'S
Journeyings.

Railways
Roman Roads
Modern Names within Parenthesis
Mr Glennie's route indicated by red line

Scale of English Miles